THE HEALING POWER
OF HUMOR

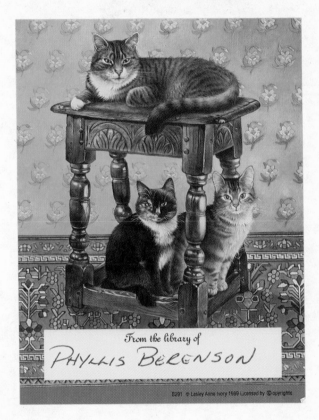

From the library of

PHYLLIS BERENSON

B291 © Lesley Anne Ivory 1989 Licensed by © opyrights

The HEALING POWER *of* HUMOR

Techniques for Getting through
Loss, Setbacks, Upsets,
Disappointments, Difficulties,
Trials, Tribulations, and All That
Not-So-Funny Stuff

ALLEN KLEIN

JEREMY P. TARCHER, INC.
LOS ANGELES

"An Autobiography in Five Chapters" used by permission of Dr. William Buchholz.

Excerpt from *Humor: God's Gift* by Tal D. Bonham, (Nashville: Broadman Press 1987) used by permission. All rights reserved.

Excerpt from the newsletter published by the American Association for Therapeutic Humor, Skokie, IL., used by permission of Alison Crane.

Excerpt from *Trinity* by Leon Uris. Copyright © 1976 by Leon Uris. Reprinted by permission of Doubleday, a division of Bantam, Doubleday, Dell Publishing Group, Inc.

The Chinese tale "The Mortal Lord" interpreted by Allan B. Chinen. Used by permission of *The Journal of Transpersonal Psychology.*

Library of Congress Cataloging in Publication Data

Klein, Allen.
  The healing power of humor / by Allen Klein.
    p. cm.
  Bibliography.
  ISBN 0-87477-519-1
    1. Laughter. 2. Wit and humor—Psychological aspects.
3. Adjustment (Psychology) I. Title.
BF575.L3K56 1988
152.4—dc19   88-19999
                                        CIP

Jeremy P. Tarcher, Inc.
9110 Sunset Blvd.
Los Angeles, CA 90069

Design by Gary Hespenheide

Manufactured in the United States of America
10 9 8 7 6 5

For Ellen,
who first showed me how to laugh,
and
for Sarah and Dave,
who continue to do so.

Contents

PART I
Learning to Laugh

PART II

When You Feel Like Crying: Techniques for Getting through Trying Times

PART III
The Last Laugh

ACKNOWLEDGMENTS

This book is not simply a marriage of me and my computer. It is the result of a collaboration of hundreds of people who have all added, in one way or another, their encouragement and inspiration to this project. Since the journey from idea to bookstore has taken me several years, I cannot possibly remember all of those who have generously shared their stories, struggles, and laughs with me. A few, however, stand out.

For their love, hugs, and support, I would first like to thank my parents, Margie and Daniel Klein; my brother, Michael Klein; my in-laws, Betty and Jim Providenty; my cousin, Bernice Shirwindt; my daughter, Sarah; and my friends Billy Cunningham, Gary Deluhery, Dorothy Duncan, and Patty Wooten. I am grateful for the suggestions of those who read early drafts of this book: Judy Tatelbaum, Willis Culver, and Barbara Iannoli. I also want to thank some of my many teachers: Dr. William Byxbee, Dr. William Fry, Jr., Lee Glickstein, Annette Goodheart, Joel Goodman, Lynn Grasberg, Stephen Levine, Dr. Virginia Tooper, and Matt Weinstein.

I am especially thankful to Michael Larsen and Elizabeth Pomada, my literary agents; Janice Gallagher, my first editor; Jeremy Tarcher, my publisher; and Hank ("More stories, more stories, more stories!") Stine.

And last, I would like to thank Dave Cooperberg, who probably read and reread this manuscript at least as many times as I did.

Allen Klein obviously has the background to teach the profound power of laughter, humor, and play. To communicate these concepts requires a maturity and an empathy that only comes from having experienced profound pain as well as profound joy. That Klein has done so is made clear in the Introduction, which lets us know from the beginning that this will not be a superficial book.

In the first part of *The Healing Power of Humor,* the author does a superb job of showing us the psychological and physiological value of laughter and play. Klein also explains many of the cultural teachings that interfere with our ability to laugh. Humor and play, the author tells us, shift our internal chemistry and profoundly impact our body's systems, including the nervous, circulatory, endocrine, and immune systems. Scientific research is helping us to understand the wise old saying, "Laughter is the best medicine."

The Healing Power of Humor also examines the importance of timing, and shows us why sometimes humor is inappropriate. As I was reading this book, I was reminded of an experience with my father shortly before he was diagnosed with an advanced malignancy. His health had been deteriorating for over a year. I went to visit him and entered his hospital room with balloons, a stick horse and all sorts of things. After we had talked a while, I began to set them up in the room. Soon he became quite agitated; it was very clear that he was upset and didn't appreciate my attempt to lighten the atmosphere.

Later that night, actually in the wee hours of the morning, my father telephoned my brother-in-law to say that I obviously didn't love him and that he was very upset. As soon as that conversation was completed, my brother-in-law called to tell me what my father had said and to ask if I thought I should do anything about it. No, I replied, feeling that my dad's reaction was due to my rather poor timing in trying to cheer him up.

The roughness and awkwardness around this episode lasted only a couple of days. I wasn't too concerned as I knew that our relationship was strong enough that this issue was essentially of little, if any, consequence—which indeed wound up being the case. However, this incident illustrates the very great risks involved in introducing humor into a serious situation.

I was aware that for over a year my father had been moving toward death. However, he was currently being evaluated for a diagnosis of medically incurable cancer. Humor was just inappropriate at that time. But this is part of the risk-taking that is necessary if we are to reap the huge benefits of laughter and playfulness when we're confronted with illness and death. We should remember that we must be willing to risk in order to grow. Laughter and play are important tools: they help us to think more creatively, to suspend limitations, and to experience the situation at hand with increased resourcefulness. As the author says, "If our attempt at humor is gentle and from the heart, the risks are minimal and basically we cannot fail."

In the second part of this book, the author gives us a number of different ways of learning to view and live through even the most trying of events. This section is full of examples and very practical suggestions that show us how to incorporate humor into our lives. This, to me, is one of the real values of the book—it enables us to look at life's difficulties from various different viewpoints.

The third part of *The Healing Power of Humor* looks at the role of humor, laughter, and play in serious illness and death. This section proved particularly helpful to me even as I was writing this foreword. I had allocated time for the task, and just when I'd reached the space I had set aside for working on it, a very special aunt died. The humor and playfulness Allen

Klein writes about were of great value in discussing death, family, burial, funerals, and so forth, and added much richness to the experience of this important time.

I am very grateful to Allen Klein for writing this book. I learned much in reading and rereading it. I recommend it to my patients and to anyone who is interested in living life more fully and more joyfully.

O. Carl Simonton, M.D.
author, *Getting Well Again*

Double Your Money

*When I'm happy I feel like crying, but when I'm sad I don't
feel like laughing. I think it's better to be happy. Then you
get two feelings for the price of one.*

—Lily Tomlin as Edith Ann

My wife, Ellen, lay dying in
the hospital, a copy of *Playgirl* by her side. Suddenly, she
opened to the male nude centerfold and insisted it be put on
the wall.

"I think it's too risqué for the hospital," I said.

"Nonsense," she replied. "Just take a leaf from the plant
over there and cover up the genitals."

I did as she requested. This worked well for the first day.
Everything was okay for the second day. By the third day,
however, the leaf started to shrivel up and reveal more and
more of what we were trying to conceal.

We laughed every time we looked at a plant or a dried-up
leaf. The duration of our levity may have lasted only ten or
twenty seconds, but it brought us closer together, revived us,
and steered us through our sea of darkness.

Humor instantly took us away, even if only for moments,
from our troubles and made them easier to bear. It gave us a
breather. It was like a minivacation that allowed us to regain
our strength and pull our resources together. Now, Ellen's
long illness was hardly a fun time; there were many tense and

tearful moments, but there were also periods of laughter. Frequently she would poke me in the ribs and admonish, "Hey, stop being so morose. I'm still here. We can still laugh together."

Ellen taught me many lessons. The most important was that we are here to have a good time. She saw every occasion as an opportunity to enjoy herself; all of the people in her life were her playmates.

Play was always an important element in her relationships. When it came time to cut the cake at our wedding and traditionally feed each other a piece of it, she knew how tense I was that day. So instead of aiming the cake for my mouth, Ellen got me to laugh by playfully aiming the cake at the top of my head.

In spite of the fact that she said I often made her laugh, it was Ellen who showed me how to do so. I am grateful for the legacy and the lessons she left me. I did not want Ellen to die, but in hindsight, I can see that her passing opened up new vistas for me that I never knew existed. Without her death, I would not be addressing thousands of people nationwide each year on the benefits of humor, nor would this book have been written.

My wife's death was an incalculable loss. But once the pain subsided and I started to accept it, my life changed dramatically. Material things had less meaning for me, my inner growth became more important; I began to understand myself and my world better. I knew I no longer wanted to continue with the work I was doing for a living, but I did not know in which direction to go. I sold my share of a silk-screen business I had owned, and I waited. I knew something would come along. Then one day a catalog from the Holistic Life University arrived in the mail. I was intrigued with the classes offered in death and dying and enrolled that very same week. Two years later, I became the director of their Life/Death Transitions program. I also became one of the first volunteers with the Hospice of San Francisco and acquired a California home health aide license.

What I observed while working with the terminally ill and the bereaved fascinated me. I saw that humor often played a big part in helping people take their minds off their distress and easing their pain.

The situations people were in were not funny themselves, but there certainly were laughs in the absurdity of some of the circumstances. One cancer patient laughed hysterically when she realized that she had spent the past months trying to decide who would get her good steak knives. And a nurse reported that she once spent forty-five minutes under a patient's bed when, moments after she accidentally fell and slid underneath it, a team of doctors and nurses surrounded the bed, their feet trapping her under it.

My awareness of the relationship between life and death grew markedly during my hospice years. The first realization was that not only will each of us have to face our own death and the loss of a loved one someday, but, in some small way, we experience loss daily. Whether our losses are the obvious ones, like a death or a divorce; not so obvious, like moving to a new home; or still less obvious, everyday occurrences, like being stuck in a traffic jam, each and every one puts us through the very same stages—anger, denial, depression, bargaining, and acceptance—that we encounter in the dying process.

I realized too that if humor helped relieve some of the distressful times associated with the death, dying, and grieving processes, then surely it was of value in such less life-threatening upsets and losses like failing an exam, burning the dinner, or being fired.

Once when I asked a nursing student, who had just failed her very first exam after getting top grades up to that point, what the worst thing was that could happen if she did not graduate, she said she did not know and became despondent. But when I continued the scenario, kidding around with her and playfully suggesting that she might meet a millionaire on the unemployment line, she chuckled and saw that failing the exam—or even not graduating—was not really the end of the world.

What disturbed me about my findings about humor was that it was rarely acknowledged as an important coping tool. In work situations, bosses often frown on employee laughter. In hospitals, nurses are reprimanded for laughing on the job, family members feel guilty for laughing around an ill loved one, and patients are accused of disrupting the routine if they are too boisterous. I thus felt a need to learn more about humor and to tell the world about its powerful potential to heal our wounds and help us deal with difficulties by giving us a new perspective on our situation. I returned to school, investigated the healing power of humor, and received a master's degree in human development from St. Mary's College in 1983. Since that time I have been writing, teaching, and speaking about why laughter is our best coping tool.

"One of the few ways to deal with a high-stress situation that you can't escape," says Dr. Samuel Shem, author of *The House of God*, "is to make fun of it." Humor helps us cope because it instantly removes us from our pain.

Besides the lessons I learned from Ellen about laughter, there was another experience that had a profound influence on the way I view the world. It came from a time when I was a scenic designer for the television show *Captain Kangaroo*. In order to create the scenery and props for the show, I had to think like a child. If Bunny Rabbit was going to build a trap to capture Mr. Moose's carrots, or if Mr. Greenjeans was creating a new invention, I had to imagine how a child would do it—probably out of Ping-Pong balls, kitchen pots, shoe boxes, ice cream cones, newspapers, old maps, or maybe even tin cans. In a child's imagination, everything and anything is possible. I also discovered that if I could capture just a small piece of this childlike vision, it would help me look at my own problems in new ways.

If I have learned anything thus far in my fifty years, it is to trust life's processes. Bad things, as a best-seller told us, happen to good people. I do not know why, nor does anyone else, but one thought has comforted me in my dark times: I have a deep belief that everything contributes to a larger, more logical picture than I can see at any given moment.

In writing this book, for example, I was upset when halfway through its completion I had a change of editors and had to rewrite most of what was already written. My initial reaction was anger and depression. But soon I saw that this was probably a blessing in disguise. I now had two points of view and two energies, male and female, contributing to and enhancing my writing.

When I can find some humor in my discomforts (like seeing the comic irony in the fact that the change of editors constituted another personal lesson in learning to laugh when I felt like crying) then I begin to see the larger picture. It expands my vision and helps me look forward instead of backward. Humor in the darkest of places is a sign of emergence from grief and depression. It is an indication that I am beginning to embrace life again and that healing is taking place.

The pain in your life comes from many places. Sometimes its source is mundane—an egg drops to the floor and it breaks. Other times its source is profound—we receive a Dear John or a Dear Jane letter and our heart breaks. Whatever our hurt, there is a big difference between pain and suffering. Our pain may not cease, but humor can minimize our suffering by giving us power in what appears to be a powerless situation.

Even in the most horrendous of circumstances, humor can impart power and help take the focus off our burdens. In his book *Man's Search for Meaning*, Viktor Frankl speaks of using humor to survive his imprisonment during World War II. He and another inmate would invent at least one amusing story daily to help them cope with their horrors. Frankl tells of the time a prisoner gestured to one of the capos (favored prisoners who acted as guards and became as arrogant as the SS men) and said, "Imagine! I knew him when he was only the president of the bank!"

I am not saying that humor is the only answer or that all of your problems will vanish if you laugh; they will not. What will result, however, when you learn to spot some humor in your difficulties, is a new perspective that will help you deal with them.

Like the spoonful of sugar in *Mary Poppins*, I believe that a bit of laughter at the right moment helps the medicine go down. After a fallen tree has landed on your car, putting a sign on it that reads COMPACT CAR may not make the car whole again, but it will help you see your misfortune a little differently.

Although my road to laughter was sparked by the death of a loved one, this book is not about death. It is about life and how to ease your problems, both the small ones and the big ones, with that healing laughter.

While I hope this book will make you chuckle from time to time, my purpose is not so much to get you to laugh (that is best left to the comedy writers) as it is to make you more aware of the humor that surrounds you (remember, the energy that created the porcupine, the platypus, and the penguin also created you), to show you where and how to find humor (have you tickled your funny bone today?), and to offer tools and techniques to help you see your pain and suffering in a new way (like exaggerating your problems and laughing at yourself before anyone else can). If, after reading this book, you can add one bit of humor to your life and your losses, I have accomplished my goal.

May you, in reading *The Healing Power of Humor*, find that, like Lily Tomlin's child character Edith Ann, you too get double your money's worth.

Enjoy!

PART

I

Learning to Laugh

A large corporation hires the Muppets to present a program explaining the company's restructuring and the possible layoff of employees. At a Texas hospital, a volunteer shows patients comedy videotapes to help reduce their pain. An East Coast prison uses cartoon therapy to assist angry inmates in dealing with the loss of their freedom. A New York doctor teaches patients to juggle in order to take their minds off their illness. A California nursing home helps residents cope with their new environment by starting an ongoing humor program.

Both medical and nonmedical settings are employing humor as a valuable resource for healing our ills, keeping us sane in an insane world and mending our losses. Humor is being used to help people adjust to their difficult and painful situations. It can also help you with yours.

Humor gives us power and a new perspective. It can help us cope and provide the strength to get through the most adverse situations. It also presents us with alternative views of our situation and keeps us in balance when our world seems to be coming apart.

Humor is an incredible, although often overlooked, tool at times when we feel like crying. "If you can find humor in anything," says comedian Bill Cosby, "you can survive it."

CHAPTER 1

What You Get
When You Laugh

Against the assault of laughter, nothing can stand.
Mark Twain

PSYCHOLOGICAL BENEFITS

HUMOR GIVES US POWER

In laughter, we transcend our predicaments. We are lifted above our feelings of fear, discouragement, and despair. People who can laugh at their setbacks no longer feel sorry for themselves. They feel uplifted, encouraged, and empowered.

Natan (Anatoly) Sharansky, the Russian human rights activist, spent nine years in Soviet prisons; included in his stay were the death sentence and sixteen months of solitary confinement. The Soviet secret police constantly threatened him with the word *rastrel*, or "firing squad." The biggest thing he had to fight, he says, was what most of us frequently battle: fear. Sharansky managed to overcome his fear and protect himself with humor. "I started talking often of the firing squad, making jokes about it. You make jokes fifteen to twenty times, and the word becomes like any other word. The ear gets accustomed to it, and it no longer prompts fear."

Instead of letting terror overcome him, which would only have made matters worse, Sharansky overcame his fears with humor. He took an intolerable situation and joked about it until it became tolerable. Often we are powerless against the events in our life; sometimes there is little we can do to stop the things that upset us. We can, however, minimize the hold that these upsets have over us by finding some humor in them. Humor can help soothe the rough edges of our day or the most trying moments of our life.

Take, for example, the eighteenth-century philosopher Moses Mendelssohn. While walking down a street in Berlin one day, he accidentally collided with a stout Prussian officer. "Swine!" bellowed the officer. Knowing that returning the insult might result in physical abuse from the officer, the philosopher opted for a different tack. He tipped his hat, gave the officer a low courteous bow, and replied, "Mendelssohn."

Humor has the power to turn any situation around.

In one of Bil Keane's "Family Circus" cartoons, we see a bathroom scene just after the toilet has overflowed. One child is wading ankle deep in water, several kids are mopping up the spill, another stands on top of the flush tank with a dripping teddy bear. In the background, an upset mother hurriedly exits the room, carrying a drenched dog. Meanwhile, the father, towels and plunger in hand, turns to his wife and says, "Look at it this way—Erma Bombeck would probably find something very amusing about this."

Comedians, cartoonists, and comedy writers know the power of humor for conquering painful circumstances. Several studies have revealed that many nationally known comedians experienced intense isolation, depression, suffering, or loss in their childhood. They found that kidding around about their losses and difficulties was a way of gaining power over them.

Both psychologist Samuel Janus and scientists Seymour and Rhoda Fisher (*Pretend the World Is Funny and Forever*) cite numerous comedians who used humor as a weapon against their pain. Totie Fields's mother died when she was five,

David Steinberg's brother was shot down in the war, Jackie Gleason's father deserted him, Joe E. Brown left his family, W. C. Fields ran away from home because his father was going to kill him, Dudley Moore was born with a clubfoot, Art Buchwald's mother died when he was very young, and Carol Burnett's parents were both alcholics who constantly fought with each other.

Charlie Chaplin, too, found solace in humor. Raised in one of the poorest sections of London, he was five years old when his father died of alcoholism; after that his mother went mad. Chaplin used these gloomy memories in his films and turned them into comedic gems. Who could forget the scene in *Gold Rush*, for example, where he eats a boiled leather shoe for dinner because no other food is available?

One of the great leaders of our country, Abraham Lincoln, lost his job, failed in business, was defeated for the legislature, lost his renomination for Congress, twice lost a bid for the Senate, and was defeated for nomination for vice-president of the United States. In spite of all the above setbacks, his bouts of depression, and the death of three sons and a sweetheart, Lincoln continually summoned his sense of humor to gain the strength and the power to go on.

In a book about Lincoln, writer Keith Jennison says that "Lincoln's ability to laugh, even during the bleakest days of the war, often astonished the people who worked with him. At one meeting during a bloody phase of the Civil War, the cabinet sat dumbfounded while he read aloud from a book of humor. After he finished he admonished the others: 'Gentlemen, why don't you laugh? If I did not laugh I should die, and you need this medicine as much as I do.'"

Laugh-makers and Lincolns live in the same painful world we all do. They also experience upsets, setbacks, and losses. One thing that makes them different from most people is that they have discovered how to turn misery into mirth and tears to laughter.

HUMOR HELPS US COPE

Nothing erases unpleasant thoughts more effectively than concentration on pleasant ones.

Hans Selye, stress researcher

In her best-selling book *Pathfinders*, Gail Sheehy discovered that the ability to see humor in a situation was one of the four coping devices that "pathfinders," people who overcome life's crises, used as a protection against change and uncertainty. (The other three coping devices were more work, dependence on friends, and prayer.) With remarkable consistency, she reports, people with high senses of well-being got through rough passages by seeing humor in difficult situations.

In another study, which spanned thirty-five years, Dr. George Vaillant, professor of psychiatry at Harvard Medical School and author of *Adaption to Life*, found similar results to Sheehy's. Along with anticipation, altruism, suppression, and sublimation, he revealed that humor was one of the five "mature coping mechanisms" used by professional men in stressful times.

Humor helps us cope with difficulties in several ways. For one, it instantly draws our attention away from our upsets. When my car radiator exploded on the highway, I managed to ease my upset by amusing myself. While waiting for a tow truck, I sat on the side of the road for three hours and built a castle out of old Coke cans, cardboard cups, and matchbooks.

Much of the suffering we experience is not a result of our difficulties but how we view them. It is not so much the actual event that causes us pain as how we relate to it.

All of us experience life's traffic jams, fender-benders, and roadblocks. For one person, the bus breaking down is a major upset; for another, it is a glorious chance to enjoy one's surroundings while walking to one's destination.

As scientists investigate the connection between the mind and the body, they are finding more and more evidence indicating that our feelings, thoughts, and attitudes not only play an obvious role in our mental health, but are also major contributors to both our physical well-being and ability to recover from illness.

Various studies have validated the mind/body connection. Hemophiliac children have actually been known to bleed not only from physical injuries but from feelings of sadness. Men who are cynical or angry have been shown to be more prone to heart attacks than those with a more positive outlook. Hospital patients who had surgery healed quicker if they had a park view out their window than those who did not.

A number of years ago, the classic stress study done by Holmes and Rahe rated the major changes in our life—both the negatives ones (death of a spouse, loss of a job) and the positive ones (birth of a child, going on vacation). It was thought at that time that the larger losses and changes in our life caused the most stress and were the greatest threat to our health. What is becoming clearer today, according to researcher Dr. Richard Lazarus of the University of California at Berkeley, is that our daily stresses unchecked over a period of time seem to be the biggest culprits and probable perpetrators of illness.

What all of these findings show is that it is of vital importance that we use a positive attitude—which a healthy sense of humor can provide—toward our stressful situations, changes, and losses. This will prevent them from manifesting into physical disorders.

By focusing our energy elsewhere, humor can diffuse our stressful events. It releases built-up tension and pops the cork off such things as fear, hostility, rage, and anger.

Fear and rage are two emotions that have been associated with heart attacks. Stanford University psychiatrist Dr. William Fry, Jr., who has done extensive research documenting the physiological benefits of laughter as well as other aspects of the humor story, notes that these emotions are countered and alleviated by humor. Fry says that humor can play a major role in maintaining a healthy heart. "Humor acts to relieve fear," he states. "Rage is impossible when mirth prevails."

Laughter releases the tension around even the heaviest of matters. At one point during the Cuban missile crisis, Soviet and American negotiators became deadlocked. There they sat in silence, until someone suggested that each person tell a humorous story. One of the Russians told a riddle: "What is the difference between capitalism and communism?" The answer? "In capitalism, man exploits man. In communism, it's the other way around." The tactic worked; with the mood relaxed, the talks continued.

Another example of how humor can relieve stress and help us cope with an upset concerns a woman who wanted to impress her clients with an elaborate dinner. She spent the entire day cooking and even hired someone to serve the meal. All went well until the main course. As they were bringing in the crown roast, the kitchen door hit the server from behind and the platter went flying across the room. The hostess froze, regained her composure, then commanded, "Dear, don't just stand there. Pick up the roast, go in the kitchen, and get the *other* one!"

Psychoanalyst Dr. Martin Grotjahn, author of *Beyond Laughter*, noted that "to have a sense of humor is to have an understanding of human suffering and misery. . . . Humor bespeaks a sad acceptance of our weakness and frustration. But laughter also means freedom." We may not actually solve our problems with humor but we may discover, at least while we are laughing, a way out. No matter if it is an embarrassing situation, a minor upset, or a major setback; if we can see some humor in it, we begin to disconnect and free ourselves from that event.

Adding humor to our difficult times can be one of the

wisest things we can do to help us cope with them, stop worrying about them, and get on with our life.

> *A rabbi who lost his entire life's savings sat reading the Torah.*
> *"I thought you were supposed to be a wise man," his wife said. "How can you sit there reading when we have lost all our money?"*
> *"I am a wise man," replied the rabbi. "I got my worries over with so that I can sit and read the Torah."*

Humor will not retrieve our losses, but it will help us get over them. Comedian Michael Pritchard equates laughter to changing a baby's diaper: "It doesn't change things permanently, but it makes everything okay for a while."

HUMOR PROVIDES PERSPECTIVE

> *Distance doesn't really make you any smaller, but it does make you part of a larger picture.*
>
> Ashleigh Brilliant,
> *I May Not Be Totally Perfect, But Parts of Me Are Excellent*

In an article in the *Journal of the American Medical Association*, Dr. Paul Ruskin demonstrated how a small humorous twist can provide an entirely new perspective. While teaching a class on the psychological aspects of aging, he read the following case study to his students:

The patient neither speaks nor comprehends the spoken word. Sometimes she babbles incoherently for hours on end. She is disoriented about person, place, and time. She does, however, respond to her name. I have worked with her for the past six months, but she still shows complete disregard for her physical appearance and makes no effort to assist her own care. She must be fed, bathed, and clothed by others. Because she has no teeth, her food must be pureed. Her shirt is usually soiled from almost incessant drooling. She does not walk. Her sleep pattern is erratic. Often she wakes in the middle of the night, and her screaming awakens others. Most of the time she is friendly and happy, but several times a day she gets quite agitated without apparent cause. Then she wails until someone comes to comfort her.

After presenting the case, Ruskin asked the students how they would like taking care of this person. Most of the students said they would not care for it at all. When he told them he would enjoy it and thought that they might too, they were puzzled. Then he passed around a photo of the patient. It was his six-month-old daughter.

Humor lends a fresh eye. It is like one of those old-fashioned topsy-turvy drawings. You hold it one way and you see a picture of a man who is sad. You turn it around, and the man's beard becomes his hair, his mustache becomes his eyebrows, and suddenly the man is smiling—the same picture, but when seen from another angle it looks entirely different. Humor approaches things sideways, upside down, backward, and inside out.

When we can find some humor in our upsets, they no longer seem as large or as important as they once did. Humor expands our limited picture frame and gets us to see more than just our problem.

Think of an upset you have experienced. Start small, like failing an exam, burning the toast, or breaking a favorite dish.

Now imagine that upset written on the palm of your hand.

Then press the palm of your hand against your nose with your fingers pointing upward. Now get up and walk around the room with your hand against your nose.

Think of each time that you can see a little humor in your upset as causing your hand to move farther away from your face and your vision to become less blocked. Your upsets are still there, but they are no longer so prominent.

Like sheep that get lost nibbling away at the grass because they never look up, we often focus so much on ourselves and our problems that we get lost because we forget to step back and see the larger picture. It is our sense of humor, as one writer put it, that provides "a God's-eye view" of our situation.

When the naturalist William Beebe used to visit President Theodore Roosevelt at Sagamore Hill, both would take an evening stroll after dinner. Then one or the other would go through a customary ritual. He would look up at the stars, saying, "That is the Spiral Galaxy of Andromeda. It is as large as our Milky Way. It is one of a hundred million galaxies. It is 750,000 light-years away. It consists of one hundred billion suns, each larger than our sun." Then silence followed. Finally, one of them would say, "Now I think we are small enough. Let's go to bed."

A very staid English lady, who had been part of one of the British Buddhist societies for many years, came one day to visit the renowned meditation teacher Achaan Chaa. She asked him all kinds of complicated questions about meditation and the Buddhist teachings known as the dharma. The teacher asked her if she had been doing much meditation practice itself. She said no, she had not had the time; she was too busy studying the dharma. Achaan Chaa looked at her and replied, "Madam. You are like the woman who keeps chickens in her yard and goes around picking up the chicken droppings instead of the eggs."

Clearly, the woman had lost all perspective as to what it meant to follow the dharma. She had been so wrapped up in studying the teachings that she forgot to practice them.

Charlie Chaplin once said, "Life is a tragedy when seen in close-up but a comedy in longshot." Mirthmyopia is perhaps today's greatest disease. We get so caught up in our everyday struggles that we forget to step back and see the comic absurdity of some of our actions.

"When my father missed a plane," says Cavett Robert, the founder of the National Speakers Association, "he caught another one. When my grandfather missed a train, he caught one the next day. Their world did not come to an end. There were other trains and other planes. Today, we miss one section of a revolving door and our entire day is shot."

I once read a letter in the newspaper that clearly demonstrated how humor helps us step back and see ourselves and our upsets in a new way. The letter went something like this:

Dear Mom and Dad,

I am sorry that I have not written, but all my stationery was destroyed when the dorm burned down. I am now out of the hospital and the doctor said that I will be fully recovered soon. I have also moved in with the boy who rescued me, since most of my things were destroyed in the fire.

Oh yes, I know that you have always wanted a grandchild, so you will be pleased to know that I am pregnant and you will have one soon.

Love,
Mary

Then the postscript:

P.S. There was no fire, my health is perfectly fine, and I am not pregnant. In fact, I do not even have a boyfriend.

However, I did get a D in French and a C in math and chemistry, and I just wanted to make sure that you keep it all in perspective.

A humorous approach frequently also reveals new insights and possible solutions to our problems. For example, bemoaning the fact that you forgot to take the chicken out of the freezer won't help it defrost any quicker when you need to start cooking it. But perhaps using your imagination and some humor will. Consider: Taking the chicken and yourself to a health club could possibly thaw two birds with one sauna.

Our culture has been classified as a left-brain society; we think in a logical and linear way. Playing around with our problems gives us more options, because we begin to also use the right hemisphere of our brain. The right brain is the more creative part and therefore shows us things we may not see when we try to look at things logically.

For example, in one of Bennett Cerf's books, he writes about a magazine that depicted a deserted farmhouse in a desolate, sand-swept field, then offered a prize for the best hundred-word essay on the disastrous effect of land erosion. Everyone who entered the contest described the same photo, and each entry was remarkably different. But the winner, a young lad from Oklahoma, gave the scene an entirely new perspective:

> Picture show why white man crazy. Cut down trees. Make too big tepee. Wind blow soil. Grass gone. Door gone. Window gone. Squaw gone. Whole place gone to hell. No pig. No corn. No pony.
>
> Indian no plow land. Keep grass. Buffalo eat grass.

Indian eat buffalo. Hide make plenty big tepee. Make moccasin. All time eat. Indian no need hunt job. No hitchhike. No ask relief. No build dam. No give dam.

White man heap crazy.

We laugh and suddenly see that photo in a new way.

How many times have you joked about something, only to find that the joke was not so far from the truth? The perspective you got from the humor also had you thinking, "Oh, so *that's* the way it is."

Julia, the mother of six children, and Samantha, who had four, were discussing their domestic problems as they sat around the kitchen table.

"Julia, I've been meaning to ask you something," said Samantha. "How in the world do you manage to get your children's attention like you do?"

"Nothing to it," answered Julia. "I just sit down and look comfortable."

In another "oh, so that's the way it is" instance, a man crossed the border with his donkey. He was searched to make sure he was not smuggling anything and then released. The next day the same man came across the border with his donkey. Rather suspicious that the man might be trying to smuggle something, having just crossed the border the day before, the guards performed a more thorough search. Not finding anything, they released the man again and he went on his way. Every day for two years the man arrived at the border with his donkey. Each day the guards became more and more suspicious that he was smuggling something, but each day's search revealed nothing, so they let him go.

Years later, after the man no longer crossed the border, one of the retired guards spotted the man at the market. "Tell me," he said, "we know you were bringing something illegally across the border, but we could never find it. What *was* it you were smuggling?"

"Since you are retired and can't arrest me, I'll tell you: It was donkeys."

Immediately we have a new understanding, a new perspective, and a new insight to the way things are.

HUMOR KEEPS US BALANCED

A person without a sense of humor is like a wagon without springs—jolted by every pebble in the road.
Henry Ward Beecher, American clergyman

"When you lose your sense of humor," says McMurphy in Ken Kesey's *One Flew over the Cuckoo's Nest*, "you lose your footing." "He knows," says one of the other characters, "you have to laugh at the things that hurt you just to keep yourself in balance, just to keep the world from running you plumb crazy."

Being out of balance can lead to both mental and physical illness. Severe stress, for example, has been linked to a number of illnesses. And people who are depressed or suicidal have also lost their balance. They have lost all perspective. They take themselves and the world so seriously and get so caught up in their dilemmas that they cannot see any way out.

Humor offers a way out before we reach such desperate states. Once we find some comedy in our chaos, we are no longer caught up in it, and our problems become less of a burden.

It has been said that the reason angels can fly is because they take themselves lightly. Well, we may not be able to physically fly, but we can certainly lighten our problems with humor and thus fly above them.

In his book *In the Presence of Humor*, clergyman E. T. ("Cy") Eberhart writes about a conversation that takes place between a young boy and his grandfather. The grandfather asks the boy about his progress in building a doghouse for his new puppy. The boy tells him that he cannot saw straight, he bends the nails when he hammers, and he often splinters the wood, but "other than that," says the boy, "I'm doing okay."

Instead of us being weighed down by the misguided saw cuts, the bent nails, and the splintered wood—which inevitably befall us throughout our life—humor keeps us in balance, lightens things up, and reminds us know that in spite of everything, we just may be doing okay.

None of us is perfect. Most of our situations are far from ideal. One of the most compassionate things we can do for ourselves is not take those imperfections too seriously. When we can find some humor in our losses, in those things that we push away, and in those bent nails and splintered pieces, then we are, as clinical psychologist Walter O'Connell points out, "honoring our imperfections and chipped edges." When we can laugh through our tears, we are being given a powerful message. Things may be bad, but they cannot be all that bad.

PHYSIOLOGICAL BENEFITS

The art of medicine consists of amusing the patient while nature cures the disease.
                                        Voltaire, French philosopher

That humor is beneficial to our physical well-being is not a new idea. Since King Solomon's time, people have known about and applied the healing benefits of humor. Proverbs 17:22 tells us, "A merry heart doeth good like a medicine"; the Greeks included a visit to the "home of comedians" as part of their healing process; and the American Ojibwa Indian tribe had clown-doctors perform antics to cure the sick. Earlier this century, Dr. James Walsh, author of *Laughter and Health*, wrote that there seems no doubt that hearty laughter stimulates practically all the large organs . . . and heightens resistive vitality against disease."

Nonetheless, despite historical and literary confirmations, it was not until Norman Cousins, former editor of *Saturday Review* and subsequently adjunct professor at the School of Medicine at UCLA, wrote about how his experience with laughter changed his life that the scientific world began to take humor more seriously.

By now, the story of how Cousins used laughter as an integral part of his healing is familiar to most people. As he reported in his book *Anatomy of an Illness*, his laughter, along with massive doses of vitamin C, helped turn the tide of a serious collagen disease, an illness of the connective tissue. "I made the joyous discovery," Cousins reports, "that ten minutes of genuine belly laughter had an anesthetic effect and would give me at least two hours of pain-free sleep."

Cousins knew about the connection between unmanaged stress and illness. He reasoned that if negative emotional states played a part in his disease, then perhaps positive emotions could help him get well. He thus turned to humor and a steady diet of comedy. He surrounded himself with such entertainment as *Candid Camera* videos, Marx Brothers films, and *Three Stooges* comedies. He also checked out of the hospital, where he was disrupting routine and making too much noise, and moved into a hotel. There, he says, he could "laugh twice as hard at half the price."

Cousins calls laughter "inner jogging." That is because when we are engaged in a good, hearty laugh, every system in our body gets a workout.

Think of the last time you had a good belly laugh, the kind where your sides hurt when you were finished. You may have bounced up and down, rocked back and forth, or doubled over from time to time. Your mouth was probably wide open in an effort to take in more air. Tears may have been streaming down your face.

That is what was happening outside your body. Inside, you were getting a workout too. Dr. William Fry, Jr., has studied and reported on many of the physical effects of laughter. He indicates that laboratory studies have shown that mirthful laughter affects most, if not all, of the major physiologic systems of the human body. Your cardiovascular system, for example, was being exercised as your heart rate and blood pressure rose and then fell again. Your heavy breathing created a vigorous air exchange in your lungs and a healthy workout for your respiratory system. Your muscles released tension as they tightened up and then relaxed again. And finally, opiates may be released into your blood system, creating the same feelings that long-distance joggers experience as "runner's high."

It has been noted that hearty laughter is very much like aerobic exercise. In fact, Dr. Fry says, those twenty seconds of guffawing gives the heart the same workout as three minutes of hard rowing.

There are also some other benefits of hearty laughter. Unlike aerobic exercise, laughter does not require special clothing, elaborate equipment, or a specific schedule to enjoy its benefits. It is accessible, convenient, and cost-free.

THE LAUGHING/CRYING CONNECTION

Laughter and tears are both responses to frustration and exhaustion. . . . I myself prefer to laugh, since there is less cleaning up to do afterward.

Kurt Vonnegut

Laughing and crying are very similar. Often derived from the same source, they both look and sound alike, and they serve many of the same functions. There is one significant difference, however, that makes laughter more powerful than tears; but before we examine this important difference, let us first look at the connections.

The poet Kahlil Gibran once wrote, "The selfsame well from which your laughter rises was oftentimes filled with your tears." Much comedic material comes out of tearful times. "When somebody steps on the bride's train or burps during the ceremony," says comedian Phyllis Diller, "then you've got comedy."

Even the lingo of stand-up comedians reveals a partnership of the comic and the not-so-comic: "I *killed* the audience" or "They *died* laughing"—not to mention the *punch* line.

The laughing/crying connection continues. We often find tears streaming down our face during gales of laughter, and frequently a hearty laugh emerges after we have had a good cry. Even facial expressions are similar; sometimes it is hard to tell whether someone is laughing or crying.

The last time you had a good cry you probably felt drained, but you probably felt better. Chances are, you also felt this way after a hearty laugh. The reason for this is another association between laughter and crying: Each provides a powerful cathartic cleansing. Each is an important mechanism for releasing stress and tension.

Tears of sorrow and tears of joy seem to be related too. Dr. William Frey II, a biochemist from Minnesota and co-author of *Crying: The Mystery of Tears*, has found that emotional tears contain a greater concentration of protein than tears that are produced by other means, such as from cutting an onion. Frey believes that tears resulting from sadness play an important part in removing harmful substances that are produced during stress.

He also speculates that the tears of laughter serve the same function as the tears of sorrow. In other words, laughter's tears may also carry away harmful toxins from the body, and the suppression of them, as in the suppression of emotional tears, increases our susceptibility to stress-related disorders.

But in spite of all the similarities, there is one big difference between laughter and crying: Laughter helps us transcend our suffering; crying does not.

Tears of sadness turn us inward; we cry and feel sorry for ourselves. Laughter, on the other hand, focuses us outward. Laughter expands our vision and gives us a new way of seeing our situation. "The laughing person," notes author Helmuth Plessner, "is open to the world." The crying person, on the other hand, only sees his world, his suffering. Perhaps this is why one Yiddish proverb has it that "laughter can be heard farther than weeping."

Tears of sorrow focus only on one aspect of our loss: our pain. They emphasize the seriousness of the situation, bind us to our suffering, and narrow our vision.

If we are overweight and cry after an eating binge, for example, we add to our suffering by feeling sorry for ourselves. We become the central figure in our own tragedy. A little self-directed humor after an eating binge ("I don't consider myself fat; I consider myself well insulated") may not make us physically lighter but it can help us become mentally lighter.

When we can allow some humor to be part of our pain, we are not as directly involved in our suffering. It is as if we put on someone else's glasses to view our situation. Everything seems familiar, but there is a slightly different look to the scene.

It is not that our pain itself has diminished; it's just that the space around it has gotten bigger. Any animal confined to a small pen will eventually become agitated and restless. It will bray, kick, and try to tear down the fence. Expand the fence, and it will be content. "To give your sheep or cow a large, spacious meadow," said one Zen master, "is the way to control him." So to quell the pain, try making the fence bigger with humor.

In encouraging the search for humor in our losses, setbacks, upsets, disappointments, difficulties, trials, tribulations, trying times, and all that not-so-funny stuff, I am in no way minimizing the value of crying. Crying is an important part of our pain, loss, and grief. It is one of the primary ways the body relieves tension when under pressure. We must give ourselves permission to cry.

Suppressed tears can linger and continue to cause problems for a lifetime; it can be detrimental to both our physical and mental health. One psychotherapist believes that a major source of violence in this country today is our inability to cry. Another researcher found that there was a close connection between those who rarely cry or have a negative attitude about crying and such illnesses as ulcers and colitis.

Crying is important and should not be suppressed. But at some point in our upsets, in our pain, continued crying may not be the healthiest thing for us. We must begin to put what we cry about in perspective so that we can get on with our life. Tears cannot do that. Humor can.

CHAPTER 2

What You Need to Know Before You Learn to Laugh

Even professional comedians don't know if their humor will work until they try it, and sometimes it doesn't.
—Ester Blumenfeld and Lynne Alpern
The Smile Connection

WHY WE DON'T LAUGH

Certain things get in the way of laughter, and certain things encourage it. But before we examine specific techniques for adding humor to your upsets, let's explore briefly some basics about why we don't laugh, how we can begin, and what we need to be aware of when going after laughter.

A man of parts and fashion is . . . only seen to smile, but never to laugh.
Lord Chesterfield, 1748

There are many deterrents to laughter: embarrassment, pain, anger, rejection, worry, anxiety, risk, fear, criticism, and more. The list is long, and it started when we were young. Many of us remember being told, "Wipe that smile off your face," "Stop smirking," or "Settle down." Often we were asked, "When are you going to grow up?" We learned that there was something wrong with laughing. Laughter meant that we were immature. Seriousness represented godliness; laughter was more the work of the devil.

In the world of adults, these laugh inhibitors continue. Our boss thinks laughter is unproductive—"Get serious or get out." We exclude laughter from our job because we consider being a banker, lawyer, teacher, or parent too serious for humor.

Beyond our jobs, such places as churches and funerals often become no-laughing-here environments. We are afraid of appearing irreverent, of not being serious enough, of offending someone, or of saying something that might be considered inappropriate.

And then there are those times when we fear that if we laugh too hard, we will lose control and not be able to regain our composure. Many times we hold back our raucous laughter because we do not like the way we sound or look when we are guffawing.

Life is filled with numerous laugh limiters, but there is one that inhibits laughter quicker than others. We often do not attempt something funny because we fear that we will appear foolish. "It could be," says Hugh Prather, author of *Notes to Myself*, "that if I were not afraid to just 'be me' I would be naturally funny. It could be that a humorous response does flick through my mind, but fear of what people might think if I just blurted out my thoughts kills it."

In times past, the fool had a revered position in the kingdom. He could do or say almost anything. And playing the fool can still add some light to our dark times. Wendy Evans, a travel agent from Northern California, relates how a bit of foolishness once saved her Christmas.

She and her husband were invited to spend the holidays with her in-laws in Southern California. She had misgivings about going, because she knew the atmosphere would be depressing. Her mother-in-law had had a stroke several years prior, and her father-in-law had been down in the dumps ever since. Wendy made an agreement with her husband that she would go only if they could really make it feel like Christmas. To ensure this, she determined that there would be a tree, a turkey, and some holiday music, but she felt that even that was not enough to cheer things up; something wacky was called for to deal with the great depression they were apt to encounter. So Wendy and her husband went to the local costume shop and rented two green elves costumes, complete with tights, tunics, bells, and large Dr. Spock ears.

Despite their fears that their foolish theatrics might backfire, the "transformation" was a triumph. At the airport and on the flight down, they watched people's joyous reactions, they handed out candy canes, and they laughed at each other. Their costumes were a big hit when they got to their destination as well. Wendy's mother-in-law actually recognized who they were, and her depressed father-in-law laughed as she had never seen him laugh before.

"There are things," it has been said, "that even the wise fail to do while the fool hits the point." As any court jester knew, playing the fool could also shed some light on the truth. In *What They Don't Teach You at Harvard Business School*, author Mark McCormack shows how one businessman made his point by suggesting an obviously foolish idea:

> Many years ago, the Ford Motor Company went through a period in which the numbers people literally took over the company and were closing plants left and right in order to cut costs. They had already succeeded in shutting down plants in Massachusetts and Texas and seemed to be relishing their newly found power.
>
> Robert McNamara, who was president of Ford at the time, called a meeting of his top executives to discuss a recommendation he had received for the closing of yet another plant. Everyone was against it, but the predictions

from the accountants were so grim that no one was willing to speak up.

Finally a salty Ford veteran by the name of Charlie Beacham said, "Why don't we close down all the plants and then we'll really start to save money?"

Everyone cracked up. The decision was made to postpone any more closings for a while, and the bean counters went back to working for the company rather than running it.

Doing or saying something foolish once in a while can both hit the nail on the head and break up tension. When we hold back from being foolish it's usually because we are unwilling to take a risk. But when you come down to it, we are all in the same boat; to one extent or another, we are all fools. As Stewart Emory says in *Actualizations*, "To be a human being is to be a latent fool. The choice we have is whether or not we are going to be practicing fools."

WHERE YOU CAN BEGIN

If you don't know where you are going, you may end up someplace else.

Laurence Peter, *The Laughter Prescription*

INTENTION

Jim Wright, a congressman from Texas and the Speaker of the House, once said, "There are a lot of things that can break apart. But if you begin with the assumption that it isn't going to work, obviously it isn't."

When we are in a feel-like-crying situation and we assume that laughter isn't going to work, then in Jim Wright's words, "obviously it isn't." If, on the other hand, our intent is to see some humor in our trials and tribulations, then we have already begun to move in that direction.

Many people believe that laughter is spontaneous, and so feel that there is nothing they can do about making it happen. Well, it *is* spontaneous, but we can nevertheless set the stage for it to occur. We can encourage or discourage it, plan for it or ignore it, be open to it or closed.

In *A Kick in the Seat of the Pants*, Roger von Oech, a pioneer in the study of creativity, writes about the importance of setting our mental channel. Although he is not specifically talking about learning to see the humorous side of things, the principle he is discussing is the same for achieving any goal:

> Take a look around where you're sitting and find five things that have blue in them. Go ahead and do it.
>
> With a "blue" mind-set, you'll find that blue jumps out at you: a blue book on the table, a blue pillow on the couch, blue in the painting on the wall, and so on. Similarly, whenever you learn a new word, you hear it six times in the next two days. In like fashion, you've probably noticed that after you buy a new car, you promptly see that make of car everywhere. That's because people find what they are looking for. If you're looking for conspiracies, you'll find them. If you're looking for examples of man's good works, you'll find that too. It's all a matter of setting your mental channel.

Our mental channel, our mind-set, our intentions steer us in the direction we want to head; in our case, it is to learn to laugh when we feel like crying. So, if we were to paraphrase von Oech's statement to meet our learn-to-laugh needs, it might look like this:

> Take a look around where you're sitting and find five things that make you smile. Go ahead and do it.
>
> With a "smile" mind-set, you'll find that things that cause you to smile jump out at you: a childhood toy, a favorite picture, your pet, and so on. In addition, when you

smile, things seem to smile back. In other words, if you look for smiles you'll find them. It's all a matter of setting your mental channel.

To help you visually see your humor intention, try drawing the following diagram:

On a piece of paper, draw two circles, side by side. The first represents your world in the past week. The second is your world as you would like it to be.

Draw a pie-shaped wedge within the first circle that shows how much play, amusement, or laughter you have had in the past week. Next, draw a pie-shaped wedge within the second circle that represents how much play, amusement, or laughter you would like in your life.

The first circle shows you where you are now. The second one indicates where you would like to be.

These circles represent your road map to your humor journey. Once you realize that your intention is to move from circle one to circle two, you have started to shift your focus in that direction.

Jim Cathcart, a professional speaker and sales trainer, tells a story about how one young man's intent was to be a top sales leader and how this lad achieved his goals. Tim was nineteen at the time when he asked Cathcart what the secret to success was. Cathcart replied that rather than being merely goal oriented, the young chap would do better to focus instead on becoming the kind of person who would achieve those goals.

About one year later, Cathcart was the master of ceremonies at an international sales banquet in the same industry that Tim had entered. The top sales leader of the year, who had competed with salespeople all around the world, was to be announced and then awarded a brand-new white Corvette. Tim turned out to be the winner. He had three times as many points as his nearest competitor.

After congratulating him, Cathcart asked Tim how he did

it. Tim replied, "I took your advice. I asked myself, How would the international sales leader do what I'm going to do? I even asked myself that question before I came to this meeting. So I booked a first-class ticket, one way. After all, the international sales leader would certainly go first class, and he would drive back home in his brand-new car."

"But you didn't know you had won," said Cathcart.

"You're missing the point," replied Tim. "If you are really going to act like the person you are trying to become, then you let the answer to the question 'How would he or she do what I'm about to do?' guide your decisions."

Like Tim, I believe in the "be/do/have" method for achieving any goal.

First, "be" what you want to have happen. If your aim is to not be so serious about life's punches, act like someone who sees the lighter side of things. Constantly ask yourself, How would the whistle-a-happy-tune person react to the situation I am in?

Then, act accordingly. "Do" what you want to have happen. You might not have much to laugh about now, but you can, as the Reverend Robert Schuller suggests, "laugh on credit." Think about what used to make you laugh and use it to trigger laughter. Realize too that things change and that the cliché about things turning out for the best is usually true.

The third step, "have," happens automatically once you have achieved the first two. Because you are already acting like a person who can laugh in difficult times, you already have what you set out to accomplish.

DON'T COMPARE, NOURISH WHAT YOU HAVE

The worst thing you can do in looking for humor is to squelch yours because you thought something was funny but nobody else did. Do not compare your humor with someone else's.

Everyone's sense of humor is different. It reflects a particular individual personality.

In 1978, *Psychology Today* magazine did a humor survey in which 14,500 readers rated thirty jokes. Not surprisingly, different people laughed at different things. "Every single joke," it was reported, "had a substantial number of fans who rated it 'very funny,' while another group dismissed it as 'not at all funny.' " What the survey clearly showed was that our funny bones are located in different places.

You, for example, might like the Marx Brothers' slapstick humor, while I prefer the more cerebral brand of Woody Allen. Others might find nothing remotely funny in the put-downs of Don Rickles but laugh uproariously at family situation-comedies like *The Cosby Show*, and vice versa.

To find out more about your own individual, unique humor profile, answer the following questions: What makes you laugh at home? At work? On TV, in the movies, in books, in cartoons? What kind of humor do you prefer? When do you laugh the most? (Under pressure? By yourself? With others?) Where do you laugh the most? (At home? At work? On vacation?) Where do you laugh the least?

Perhaps you have discovered something about your own sense of humor you were not otherwise aware of. For example, maybe you realized that it is your eight-month-old golden retriever puppy who makes you laugh the most. Knowing this, when you get into feel-like-crying situations, take a minute or two and go and play with him or her. When you are away from home, carry a photo of that puppy around with you. That way, you can at least get a smile during those not-so-good times simply by remembering the oh-so-good times you have together.

Try and maximize those things that help you to laugh and minimize the rest. Suppose, for example, you found out from the humor profile quiz that the TV show *The Golden Girls* is what you laugh at most. Then make sure you watch it each week; videotape it if you are not home, or tape the entire series and turn it on whenever you need a laugh.

TODAY'S UPSETS ARE TOMORROW'S LAUGHS

In looking for humor, keep in mind another guideline: Sometimes it takes a little time to see the humor in your upsets; you may not find something to laugh about immediately.

H. G. Wells once said, "The crisis of today is the joke of tomorrow." Some of our most trying moments turn into laughing matter when we look back at them. Things that seemed unbearable at one time often turn out, in hindsight, to somehow have humor in them after all.

Erma Bombeck, the First Lady of household comedy, admits that it often takes a second glance at our problems before we see the humor in them. "I can't tell you how many times I've slammed the doors and thrown myself on the bed," she relates, "and I'm calling convents at two in the morning and saying, 'Take me, please.' It's only in retrospect that it has any humor whatever."

Bombeck elaborates on this in an interview written by Nanci Hellmich for *USA Today*. "When I had a cold it was absolutely tragic. I knew I was going to the big utility room in the sky. I got so sick of seeing this woman on television saying, 'Don't hate me for being beautiful.' You feel so ugly when you have a cold—your nose is running, your hair won't curl. But today it seems ridiculous. You need that time span to get a perspective."

Imagine, if you would, that today is the day you begin your two-week summer vacation. You are doing some last-minute packing while running the bath water for your four-year-old daughter; your husband is securing some boxes on top of the car. One more trip to the apartment should be all it takes to complete the car loading.

Then, just as you and your husband are moving the final piece of luggage into the hallway, the door slams shut, leaving you keyless outside the apartment with your daughter and the running bath water inside. As if the situation weren't already bad enough, the sky suddenly opens up and lets loose a torrential summer downpour. In an instant, you realize that the boxes on top of the car will soon have the consistency of tea-soaked graham crackers, the apartment below yours will soon look like Lake Erie, and your daughter will soon become the next Esther Williams.

Is this material for laughter or not?

Perhaps not at the very instant it is happening; but two seconds later, after you have figured out how to get into your apartment, why not? And two days later? Who knows? You just may find yourself doubling over with laughter when your daughter wants to know when she can play lock-me-in-the-house again.

Throughout college I had a part-time job at a concession in the Broadway theater where the show *My Fair Lady* was playing. One evening I was assigned the balcony refreshment stand. I could hear the concluding music of the first act as I made my way up the two flights of steps with a tray of thirty cups of grape juice in one hand and twenty cartons of candy-coated almonds in the other. Suddenly I missed the top step and fell. Just as the intermission crowd was entering the balcony lobby, I looked back to see a waterfall of cascading grape juice and hundreds of almonds jauntily bouncing down the steps.

At the time: cringing and humiliation. But looking back? I still chuckle at the preposterous picture.

Sometimes it takes ten seconds to see some humor in your dilemmas, sometimes ten years. The gap between your upset and the period when humor becomes obvious varies greatly, but you can shorten that gap: The next time you find yourself in a troublesome situation, stop for a moment and ask yourself what will it look like in a month, in six months, in a year, or when you are eighty-five. If you can remember to say "Some day I might laugh at this," you will be closer to doing so.

HOW TO MINIMIZE YOUR HUMOR RISKS

In matters of humor, what is appealing to one person is appalling to another.
Melvin Helitzer, author of *Comedy Writing Secrets*

Humor is risky business.

We never really know how people will react to our antics, and they never know how we will react to theirs. When dealing with people who are in the midst of a difficult passage, even more risk is involved, it being such a vulnerable time.

Humor has so much force that it can help communicate and connect—or, just as easily, destroy relationships and divide. Most memorable television commercials communicate their message with humor in less than thirty seconds (remember the "Where's the beef?" commercial?); in that same thirty seconds one ethnic joke can antagonize an entire group.

The humor used when we want to hurt someone is often put-down humor. It judges others, tries to boost the ego of one person over another, and creates ill-will instead of goodwill. It comes from a closed heart. Its I-am-better-than-you attitude creates separation and suffering.

Laughing at someone in pain is indeed inconsiderate. It only increases suffering and creates separation. Laughing with another at a painful target, on the other hand, is another matter. It is compassionate and connecting. If our attempt at humor is gentle and from the heart, the risks are minimal; we cannot fail.

If we are to gain anything from humor, we must be willing to risk. Our humor attempts may make us feel foolish or embarrassed, and they may even backfire from time to time, but as poet T. S. Eliot reminds us, "Only those who risk going too far can know how far one can go."

In spite of all the risks, one can minimize them by assessing the situation, testing the waters, and establishing rapport. Moreover, chances are that the more often you take a risk, the easier it is to try again and the more likely you are to succeed.

Before taking any potent medicine, you must read the label and follow the guidelines if you are to get the benefits and avoid the risks. Humor is no different.

ESTABLISH RAPPORT

To encourage laughing *with* people, not *at* them, we need to establish a rapport with them and give them clues that it is okay to joke around with us. We can do this with verbal clues (as when I kid around about not having much hair on my head) or nonverbal ones, as in the example that follows.

A few years ago, I had the privilege of watching a young man dressed as a clown make the rounds at a hospital. Dr. Balloon's main job was to brighten up the adult patients. I watched as he looked for clues to see if people were ready for his silliness. Was the door to the room open or closed? Were the shades or curtains drawn? Did they smile when he peeked into the room, or did they return to their book? Without much verbal contact, he could tell who was ready for some cheering up and who was not.

One day Dr. Balloon (also known as Terry McLarnan) was assigned a patient in a two-bed room. After working with her he then carefully looked for clues from her roommate to see if she was ready to join in the merriment. When he blew his "ultrasound" horn for the first patient, he poked his head around the curtain of the second and said, "I hope we're not making too much noise." From her inquisitive "No, what are you doing?" he knew she was ready to participate. He brought her some flowers to smell and then read get-well cards out loud to both of them.

Because we never really know other people's experiences, there is always some risk involved when we joke around with them. One way to minimize this humor risk is to establish a rapport. Before you start, try and find out who she is, what she laughs about, what she finds funny. Then test the waters with some trivial matter and watch what kind of reaction you get.

Patty Wooten, a nurse friend, does this when she is delivering a meal to a patient who is on a liquid diet. She might say, "Today I know we have one of your favorites. Cream of nothing soup." This may not be fall-off-your-chair-roll-on-the-floor humor, but if she gets a chuckle, or even a smile, she knows she can go ahead with some other lighthearted comments.

A good rule of thumb in looking for clues to other people's sense of humor is to listen to what they say. At an international meeting of top-ranking company officials, one executive from America asked another executive from Japan what the Japanese regarded as the most important language for world trade. The American thought the answer would be English, but the executive from Japan smiled and replied, "My customer's language." We need to listen to what other people say, and sometimes even read between the lines.

Do you know someone who jokes about taxes or their run-down car? Chances are that it is relatively safe for you to kid around about those things too. On the other hand, do you work with someone who laughs about his big nose? Or do you have a friend who jokes about never being married? Beware. It may be okay to join in, it may not. Even if they joke about themselves, the more personal the joking, the more caution you need to take.

APPROPRIATE VERSUS INAPPROPRIATE HUMOR

Whether you are using humor to ease your own dilemma or someone else's, the best rule to use is the AT&T principle: Make sure it is appropriate, timely, and tasteful.

There is a fine line between when humor is appropriate, timely, and tasteful and when it is not. What offends one person might amuse another.

Patty, the nurse just mentioned, shared a story with me about how the same bit of humor was appropriate in one case and offensive in another. She was bathing a hospital patient who had a rather large surgical scar. The woman chuckled when Patty noticed it and said, "My scar looks just like San Francisco's Market Street, doesn't it." Not understanding what the woman meant, Patty asked, "How so?" She replied, "Well, it goes all the way from Twin Peaks to the waterfront." They both laughed uproariously, and Patty continued the bath.

About a year later, Patty encountered another woman with a similar scar. Thinking she could cheer this person up she said, "That scar looks just like Market Street in San Francisco." When Patty explained why, the woman became highly insulted.

Although the circumstances were similar, the first bit of humor came from the injured; the second from an outsider. The first woman felt comfortable enough with what she had experienced to be able to laugh about it; the second woman did not. Again, we need to listen carefully to what people say; then—and only then—consider whether or not it is safe to jump in and continue to kid around about the same thing.

HUMOR: HANDLE WITH CARE

There is always some risk in attempting humor—sometimes it backfires. For example, a radio disc jockey reported that at work one night he accidentally knocked the record player, sending the needle screeching across the record. To ease his error, he immediately grabbed the microphone and shouted, "Okay—which one of you listeners out there bumped into your radio and made my record skip?" To his embarrassment, several people actually phoned the radio station to apologize.

Many years ago, one of my very first jobs was designing window displays for a suburban branch of Macy's department store. One Christmas season, we put huge cabinets in each window and then filled them with merchandise. It was getting late, and we were nowhere near finished. Looking around at my stressed co-workers, I decided it was time for a little humor.

I climbed into one of the cabinets and sat cross-legged inside. When anyone passed the window, my two co-workers would open the double doors of the cabinet and I would bow. Then my cohorts would close the doors and go about their business as if nothing had happened. After several of these appearances, the doors once again opened. I took a slow, deep bow, and upon coming up opened my eyes to discover my boss staring into the window, sternly shaking his head from side to side.

I did not get fired, but it was my first and last live window performance.

JOKES ARE ONLY A SMALL PART OF HUMOR

There are two reasons for being cautious about using jokes as your main humor source: First, most of us cannot tell a joke well, and second, jokes are often offensive.

Jokes frequently ridicule, tease, insult, and degrade. Blue jokes, for example, can embarrass and exploit, sick jokes can be repulsive, and ethnic jokes perpetuate stereotypes. Before telling a joke, try to know your audience. It is safe, for example, to tell an ethnic joke to people of that background if you are one of them; it probably is not if you are not.

And then, good joke telling takes talent, timing, and lots of practice—which most of us do not have. To wit:

A group of prisoners had been in prison together for such a long time that instead of repeating the same jokes over and over again, they would assign each joke a number and then call out that number when they wanted to tell a joke.

One day, a prisoner called out, "Nine," and everybody got hysterical.

Another inmate topped that with, "Six," and the entire cell block broke up with laughter.

Finally, a third inmate shouted out, "Four," but nothing happened; there was dead silence.

When he asked his cell-mate why everybody had laughed when the others had called out a number but nobody laughed when he did, his partner replied, "Some people just don't know how to tell a joke."

You can reduce the risks of joke telling by steering away from potentially offensive jokes and by practicing. To do this, tell one joke a week to as many people as you can. At the end of a week, you will know one joke. At the end of the month, four. By the end of the year, you will know fifty-two.

The joke I am currently practicing is: "I recently had an opportunity to use the telephone they now have on airplanes. I called out for a pizza."

Remember, it is all right not to tell jokes. They are, after all, only a small part of humor. There are many other nonjoke ways of adding humor to your life and your difficult situations, as we will see in the pages that follow.

PART

II

When You Feel Like Crying: Techniques for Getting through Trying Times

If this were a diet book, it might have been called *Two Weeks to a Lighter You.* The reason for that is that if you incorporate into your life each day one of the fourteen techniques that follow, by the end of two weeks you will have shed some pounds of excess gloom.

As you read on—and, I hope, as you try the exercise that follows each technique—you may come up with your own angles on how to add humor to your life and your losses. Surely there are many more suggestions and possibilities that have not been included. But the ones that are here will doubtless help you start to see your trying times in a new way.

As you experiment with these ideas, remember to take your time and be patient with yourself. Change is hard. It takes time. It does not happen overnight.

All of the techniques here are user friendly. They appear in a certain order because some seem more closely related than others, but the order you choose to practice them is not important. What does matter is that you consciously focus on one of these techniques each day.

Think of these fourteen ideas as you would your morning vitamins. Vitamin H is for Humor. Make sure you get your daily dose.

Spotting Life's Setups,
or
How to Keep an Elephant
from Charging

When you get to the end of your rope, tie a knot and hang on. And swing!

Leo Buscaglia

In every job, relationship, or life situation there is inevitably some turbulence. Learn to laugh at it. It is part of what you do and who you are.

If you are a baker, chances are you will burn a few cakes every now and then. If you are a homemaker, you will break a few dishes from time to time. If you are a clerk at a supermarket, there is a great possibility that one day one of the grocery bags will burst as you finish filling it. You can be prepared, as one clerk was, with, "They just don't make these bags like they used to; this was supposed to happen in your driveway!"

You cannot expect things to run smoothly twenty-four hours a day, 365 days a year, for your entire life. Why not prepare for those rough spots before they occur and be ready with some way to lighten them up?

Most of us can laugh at the punch line of a joke, but few laugh at life's punches. Life, however, is similar to the structure of a joke. In life, we think we are heading in one direction, as in the unfolding of a joke, and then fate, like the punch line, takes us down a different path.

The setup of a joke might be, "How do you keep an elephant from charging?" The shift of focus, from a large animal attacking us to something entirely different, happens in the punch line: "Take away his credit card."

Learn to keep an eye out for the setup. Then at least when the trouble strikes you will be ready to meet the disturbance with your own punch line.

In life, a setup might be that your boss has rejected your budget proposal for the fifth time this week. You feel frustrated because of the time you lost in redoing that budget over and over again. Maybe you even feel some loss of self-confidence; can you really get the job done?

This punch line was effective for one businesswoman: She took her unacceptable budget to the copy machine and made it the size of a postage stamp. Then she presented it to her boss as her "reduced budget."

It is impossible to anticipate all of the daily problems you might encounter, but there are certain ones that you know will occur because of the nature of your profession or circumstances. Having anticipated this setup, you can be ready with a stock punch line. One husband, for example, knew that every year on the family's way to their vacation spot, just as they would get about eighty miles out of town, his wife would cry out, "Oh, no! I'm sure I left the iron on." Each year they would return home only to find it unplugged. One year, however, was different; the man had anticipated what was coming. When his wife gasped, "We must go back, I just *know* I left the iron on," he stopped the car, reached under his seat, and handed his wife the iron.

If you are a nurse you know that sooner or later a doctor will become upset and perhaps shout at you. To disarm this encounter, one nurse relates how she and her co-workers have a nurses' agreement: If one nurse sees another being reprimanded by a doctor, she calls out, "Code nurse," and they all circle silently around the couple.

If you drive a car, you know that someday you might be stopped by a police officer. Are you ready for it? One person was. When asked for her license, she handed it to the officer along with an orange card from her Monopoly game. It read GET OUT OF JAIL FREE.

Of course, you cannot anticipate every one of life's setups, but you do not have to in order to be ready with a punch line. Most crises and setbacks provide a calm after the storm, a moment in which you can catch your breath and devise a punch line before anything else happens.

As a professional speaker, I know that not every one of my presentations will be perfect. I know that things might happen that I have little or no control over, but I also know that I can soften them with humor.

During one presentation, all the lights went out as I was speaking. I continued my talk and informed the audience that I would now be speaking about "black humor." At the start of another program, the fire alarm sounded just as I said, "And my joke for this week is . . ." At first the audience laughed, thinking it was part of my routine; I even thought someone might be playing a joke on *me*. When I realized that this was not the case, I instructed the audience to head for the exits. And I began to look for the punch line. Soon we learned that it was a false alarm, and everyone returned. As I welcomed them back to "the second half" of my talk, I noted that humor is such a hot topic it sets off alarms.

Another professional speaker, Michael McKinley, was addressing a group while a torrential rainstorm proceeded outside. Suddenly water started seeping through the doors. Thinking quickly, he calmed the audience's fears and made a bad situation pay off: "Attention! Attention!" he announced. The lifeguard will be giving swimming lessons in the lobby in half an hour." At the end of his presentation he added, "Thank you for inviting me to speak to you tonight. The ark will be leaving in a few minutes."

In his book *Oops! Or Life's Awful Moments*, radio and television personality Art Linkletter relates how he used humor in one of the greatest public catastrophes that ever occurred to him. He was to speak before a very large audience that was gathered together for one of the first Emmy Award programs televised coast to coast. Just as he said, "Good evening, ladies and gentlemen," the master light switch exploded, leaving everyone in total darkness. He reports, "Stagehands began running in all directions, knocking the entire Grecian set down. Walls, pillars, and great façades tumbled onto the orchestra. One entire section of strings was knocked out by an enormous pillar." With time to think, when the lights returned, Linkletter slowly surveyed the wreckage and then announced, "For an encore, ladies and gentlemen, we will now set fire to Lucille Ball."

Your own mishaps may not occur in front of hundreds of people, but no matter what your situation, the solution remains the same: Be ready to poke fun at your minor mishaps and you can survive them. What a great line Linkletter gave all of us to use at such times when we have spilled coffee all over our desk, locked our keys in the car, or dropped the groceries. "For an encore, ladies and gentlemen, I will now..."

Recently it seems that airline employees use what sounds like prepared humor to diffuse the tension around the hassles and mishaps inevitably encountered in flying. One time, a pilot who made a very hard landing apologized with this explanation: "There was the cutest little rabbit crossing the runway just as I was about to land, so I bounced over it. Now you wouldn't want me to hit that rabbit, would you?" One flight attendant was heard to calm down some disgruntled passengers by announcing, "Federal regulations require that all luggage fit under your seat or be jammed into the spacious overhead bins."

Rudolf Bing, who was the general manager of the Metropolitan Opera for many years, disliked having to negotiate with the trade unions. He knew that it was a time for much hysteria and confrontation. So one session he came prepared: Leaning across the table toward the union's lawyer, he responded "I'm awfully sorry, I didn't get that. Would you mind screaming it again?"

Many people seem to habitually lose such small items as keys, wallets, and umbrellas. If you are one of them, you might want to have a little humor ready for the next time. I know several instances in which humor not only eased the loss but actually helped retrieve the items.

Dr. Virginia Tooper, editor of *Laugh Lovers News* and founder of Sarcastics Anonymous, was successful in recovering several pairs of lost glasses by attaching this note inside her glass case:

> If you have these, I don't. They were lost by a sweet little old lady who is now driving home without them . . . somewhere in this area . . . amongst your loved ones. Please call the number below and do yourself and everyone within a hundred miles a *big* favor.

A story in *Funny Funny World* told of a Long Island commuter who was constantly leaving his umbrella on the train or in a restaurant. His wife attached this message to it: "If found, do not attempt to return. Instead, keep and send three dollars to buy a new one." Six months later she had forty-five dollars in three-dollar checks.

A bit of preplanned humor for potential upsets and losses is like having a psychological insurance policy: You may never need it, but it sure is nice to know it's there if you do.

LEARN-TO-LAUGH EXERCISE

Some days are better (or worse) than others. Like the Boy Scouts, be prepared! Look for the setups of life and be ready to handle them with humor. When you encounter one of those not-so-great times, have a funny familiar punch line ready. Use it like a humor mantra, which you can repeat to yourself or out loud, depending on the company you keep.

Make up your own or use some of these classic lines that have helped thousands of others:

"Oh, what an opportunity for growth and learning."

"It could be worse. I could be pregnant."

"If it's not one thing, it's another."

"Take it back. It's not what I ordered."

"I'd rather be —— (dancing, skiing, jogging, and so on).

"Don't ask me, I only work here."

"Here we go again."

"I have no time for a crisis, my schedule is full."

"I refuse to be intimidated by reality."

"Beam me up, Scotty."

Joke-Jitsu

Playwright George Bernard Shaw once wrote to Winston Churchill:

Dear Mr. Churchill,
Enclosed are two tickets to my new play, which opens Thursday night. Please come and bring a friend, if you have one.

To which Sir Winston replied:

I am sorry, I have a previous engagement and cannot attend your opening. However, I will come to the second performance, if there is one.

In jujitsu, the Japanese martial-arts form, you gain an advantage over your opponent by turning his strength and weight against him. Humor, too, can take any upsetting situation and turn it into an advantage. By giving the situation a twist, humor reverses the energy and sends it spinning in the opposite direction. I call this joke-jitsu.

Joel Goodman, director of the Humor Project, illustrates joke-jitsu (which he calls aikido humor) with a story about how Eve Arden, the actress who portrayed Miss Brooks on TV, dealt with a practical joke that was sprung on her the closing night of one of her stage performances. Arden's costar had the sound man ring the prop telephone in the middle of her monologue at a time not specified in the script. When the phone rang, Arden picked it up, paused, and then handed it to her leading man. "It's for you," she said.

In his quarterly magazine, *Laughing Matters*, Goodman shares another joke-jitsu anecdote about a policeman who was being considered for a promotion to captain. During one of his interviews, the cop was tossed a curveball, a trick question:

> "Suppose you were involved in a high-speed chase. The car you were chasing sped through the intersection ahead, and then all of a sudden, a big battleship moved across the intersection, blocking your way. What would you do?" The man responded with, "Of course I'd sink it!" The interviewers were taken aback and asked, "Just how would you sink it?" The interviewee quickly replied, "With my submarine!" Astonished, the interviewers pushed further. "And where did you get the submarine?" At this point, the interviewee pulled out his final ace and said, "The same place you got your battleship!"

Sir Winston Churchill, as evidenced by the quote at the beginning of this section, was a verbal martial-arts master. Once, Churchill and Lady Astor were discussing the role of women in Parliament, a subject she strongly believed in and Churchill opposed. Somewhat frustrated with the conversation, Lady Astor said in exasperation, "Sir Winston, if I were your wife I would put arsenic in your coffee." To which Churchill *replied,* "Madam, if I were your husband, I'd drink it."

During his last year in office, Churchill attended an official ceremony. While there, he heard two men behind him whispering. "That's Winston Churchill. They say he is getting senile. They say he should step aside and leave the running of the nation to more dynamic and capable men." When the ceremony was finished, Churchill turned around and said, "Gentlemen, they also say he is deaf."

Several presidents of the United States have also perfected their agility at martial-arts humor. One of them was President

Reagan. When derogatory comments were made about his age during his second bid for the Oval Office, he answered his critics, "Andrew Jackson was seventy-five years old and still vigorous when he left the White House. I know, because he told me."

Another time, Reagan said, "I will not make age an issue of this campaign. I am not going to exploit, for political purposes, my opponent's youth and inexperience."

Like martial arts, humor can turn around any disagreeable situation, diffuse an attack, and disarm the attacker. When two tough-looking men demanded money from a marine, he used his recruiter's pitch to halt the altercation. "Fellows," he said, "this might be your lucky day. The United States Marine Corps is looking for determined, forceful individuals just like yourselves. How would you like to serve your country?" The two thugs turned and ran as quickly as they could.

One writer, tired of getting one rejection slip too many, replied to yet another with one of his own. He wrote back to a magazine that had not accepted his article, "We are sorry to inform you that your rejection slip does not meet our editorial needs."

Here is how Robert Farmer, head of an advertising and public relations firm, turned a potentially nasty situation around with humor. It seems that on both sides of the building he had purchased for his business's relocation there was an auto painting shop that used the area in front of his building for a driveway and parking lot. After asking them to cease, to no avail, he blocked the path with seven oversized concrete pots containing large evergreens. This, of course, stopped all vehicular traffic but also increased hostility.

Shortly after the installation of the urns, Farmer noticed that the evergreens were turning brown. Upon closer examination, he found that the soil smelled of gasoline. After considering all legal, authoritarian, and vengeful avenues, he instead opted for humor. He sent a letter to the company next door: "Tell your boys who are putting gas in our plants out front to use unleaded; they'll run better that way!"; he also stuck small signs in the plants that read UNLEADED ONLY, PLEASE!

Take a really tough situation: Suppose you found that your boss was opening and reading your personal mail. How might a knowledge of joke-jitsu help?

Communication specialist and humorist Bob Ross tells his story of this happening in a company for which he worked. He turned this on itself by sending other employees very cryptic letters marked "personal and confidential." These letters would include espionage-type language, such as "Meet me under the bridge after work; I have the money and the plans." He would sign the letter with a fictitious name and then watch with glee as his boss opened and read the phony note.

In *How to be Funny*, comedian Steve Allen writes about how he used humor to turn around a potentially embarrassing situation on his radio show:

Jim Moran, the advertising and promotional genius, was on, pushing Persian rugs. He entered, dressed as an Arab, leading an enormous camel. Well, right in the middle of our conversation, the camel began to urinate all over the linoleum floor. Camels have a tremendous capacity to store water, of course, so when they empty their bladders, it takes a while—much longer than for, say, a horse or an elephant.

Anyway, the audience got hysterical. So Jim and I stopped the conversation. The camel went on for about five minutes. The longer he relieved himself, the more the audience laughed. Stagehands came out with buckets and mops to clean up the mess, which was about to spill out into the audience.

After everything was mopped up, the linoleum—originally a dark brown color—was about eight shades lighter, since the waxy buildup, or whatever, had been removed. It had now been reduced to a pale shade of yellow. Suddenly, that transformation struck me funny and I said: "Say, home-makers, having trouble keeping kitchen floors spotlessly clean?"

The laughter was loud and long.

A final story of how humor can turn difficulties around comes from the Yiddish tradition.

There once dwelled a rabbi with such a golden voice that everybody clamored to hear him. In each city he visited, women would shower him with flowers and merchants would ply him with gifts.

One day the rabbi's faithful sleigh driver said, "Rabbi, for once I'd like to be the one receiving all the honors and attention. Just for tonight," the driver suggested, "change clothes with me. You be the driver and I'll be the rabbi."

The rabbi agreed but added, "Remember, clothes do not make the man. If you're asked to explain some difficult passage of the Talmud, see that you don't make a fool of yourself."

The exchange occurred. When the two men arrived at the next town, the bogus rabbi was received with much enthusiasm and obviously enjoyed it. Moreover, since the driver had heard the rabbi's speech hundreds of times, he delivered it perfectly.

Then the dreaded question-and-answer period came. An aged scholar arose and asked a rather difficult and tricky question. The real rabbi in the back of the room thought, "Now he'll make a fool of himself."

But the driver managed to turn the punch around. "A fine scholar you are! Why, your question is such a simple one that even the old uneducated fellow who drives my sleigh must know the solution. Driver, come up here to the platform and answer this poor fellow!"

LEARN-TO-LAUGH EXERCISE

This joke-jitsu exercise will help you turn upsetting situations into humor.

There is the standard joke setup using a "good news/bad news" formula. I am sure you have heard some of them, but here is an example: "The good news is your wife found a photo worth over one hundred thousand dollars. The bad news is that it's of you and your secretary."

Try lightening your problems by reversing the "good news/bad news" formula. State your bad news first and then turn it into good news. For example:

"The bad news is that we had a flood at the warehouse this weekend. The good news is the water is being diverted into a new employee swimming pool."

"The bad news is that my suitcase fell apart as it came off the airplane. The good news is that it was the first out of the baggage chute."

"The bad news is that my husband ran off with my best friend. The good news is that I now have two fewer people to buy Christmas presents for."

Exaggerate!!

I wouldn't say the rooms in my last hotel were small, but the mice were hunchbacked.

Fred Allen

Exaggeration is one of the simplest techniques for making our painful moments laughable. It is the art of reframing our difficulties and disappointments so that they hurt less. When we are blinded by our upsets, when they are all we can see, sometimes describing them in highly dramatic or overinflated terms can allow us to see the ludicrousness of our situation.

Exaggeration is such a powerful tool for providing a perspective in times of tears that it has become an important part of such mental-health approaches as Provocative Therapy and Rational Emotive Therapy. Both Frank Farrelly and Albert Ellis, respective founders of these therapy practices, use exaggeration to show their clients that sometimes serious problems can be taken too seriously.

In his book *Making Things Better by Making Them Worse*, Dr. Allen Fay also shows people how they can overcome their problems by exaggerating them. Often, he says, the harder we try to get rid of our problems, the more difficult it is. On the other hand, by exaggerating them we start to see their absurdity, get a new perspective, laugh, and let go. In the following example, Fay illustrates how one wife used exaggeration to successfully communicate with her husband:

A young married man who lived in New York had an older sister in California who often took advantage of him. Although she was very wealthy and he was not, she would call him long distance and expect him to return her call if he was not in. She would then keep him on the phone for long periods of time, thus running up large bills for him. His wife resented the situation and often nagged him not to allow his sister to exploit him. He would become defensive, and a fight would usually be the outcome.

On one occasion, when he came home his wife said, "Your sister called earlier today and wants you to call her back." The young man was about to go to the phone when his wife continued, "I don't think you should call her; instead, why not be a really good brother and fly out to California. I'll drive you to the airport and you can be in California later tonight." The husband was amused and said, "I'll wait for her to call me again."

Once, in a store, I saw a customer hand the clerk a $100 bill to pay for his $9.95 purchase. The clerk explained that she did not have change. She apologized, said she had just opened the shop, and suggested that the man go to the bank down the block and get smaller bills. The customer was unwilling to do this and insisted, in a rather loud voice, that the clerk go to get the change. When the clerk said she could not leave the store, the man's verbal attack intensified. Finally he stormed out. Seeing the distress in the clerk's face and the tears in her eyes when I went to pay for my 85-cent purchase, I stepped up to the counter, opened my wallet, and exclaimed, "Oh, my god, I only have a $1,000 bill!" The clerk laughed and calmed down.

The following lesson illustrates how exaggeration can be used to improve any situation. My friend's mother used to tell it whenever anyone complained. The tale concerns a man who went to the rabbi to lament about the crowded conditions in his house.

"Rabbi," said the man, "My house is so small. With my wife, my children, and my in-laws living in one room, we are always getting in each other's way. We are always yelling at one another. I don't know what to do."

The rabbi asked the man if he had a cow. When the man answered that he did, the rabbi advised the man to move the cow into the house.

Perplexed, the man did as he was told but returned a week later to report that things were even more unpleasant than before. "Move your two goats into the house also," the rabbi advised. Once again the man followed the rabbi's advice but again returned to declare that the situation was worse.

Again the rabbi asked the man what animals he had.

When the man answered that he also had a dog and some chickens, the rabbi told him to put those in the house too and return in a week. Bewildered, the man went home and followed the advice of the scholar.

This time when the man returned, he was screaming. "It is unbearable. I've got to do something. I am going out of my mind. Please help me."

"Listen carefully," said the rabbi. "Take the cow and put it in the barn. Move the goats into the yard. Put the dog outside. And return the chickens to the coop. Then come back to see me in a few days.

When the man returned, he was elated. "Oh, Rabbi," he said, "with only my wife, my children, and my in-laws in the house, there's so much room. What an improvement!"

When my own daughter was a teenager, she would sometimes complain that she had no Saturday-night date. Here it was, all-American date night, and she was home alone. After her moaning and groaning went on for some time, I would join her and begin to exaggerate the results of being dateless. "Sarah, this is terrible. This is a tragedy. My life is ruined. Here it is Saturday night and both of us have not been invited anywhere. What are we going to do?'' Eventually Sarah would giggle at my antics and realize that the evening was not a total loss; we then could either do something together or entertain ourselves alone.

A woman friend of mine would use exaggeration to diminish her husband's rage whenever her credit card purchases were too high. She would tell him that as she was walking down the street a huge gust of wind had come up behind her and blown her through the Bloomingdale's revolving door. The wind was so great that it swept her up the escalator to the third floor. There the blast of air threw an expensive dress at her, causing a chain reaction. Her purse landed on the counter, her wallet fell out, and her credit card popped into the hands of a waiting clerk.

Exaggeration can take many forms. One that can be most useful in dealing with upsets is to write an overstated letter. You do not need to mail it. Just putting your exaggerated feelings on paper will frequently turn your hurt into humor and help ease your pain.

A few years ago, I recall relieving my own anger over a high medical bill by writing the following:

Dear Doctor,

I recently received your bill for my daughter's annual checkup. The unexplained seventy-five-dollar figure floored me.

After getting up from the floor, I called your office for an itemization. I was told that Sarah was older and bigger, so the bill was higher.

Does this mean that she has more to examine now? Do you charge by the square inch? If the bill is higher because she is older, than how come my doctor only charges me thirty-five dollars and I am forty-five?

Fear not. I intend to pay your bill. If for no other reason than I would not have to look at those shocking-pink stickers month after month informing me of my delinquency.

As a matter of fact, I think I have just touched upon why your fee is so high. Those shocking-pink stickers are expensive. I remember those cheaper, old-fashioned white ones with glue that came off on your tongue.

But then, those were the good old days when doctors made house calls and did not charge by the size of the patient.

I sent the doctor the letter and never heard from him again. I also changed doctors; after all, who wants a doctor without a sense of humor? Actually, I think I got the last laugh—his name was Dr. Graves.

The *New York Times* once published an exchange of exaggerated letters between a man and his neighbor:

Dear John,

I have been very impressed over the past four or five weeks how smart your dog, Prince, is. "How does Ed know our dog is so smart?" you are asking yourself. Well, I know he is smart because he reads the *New York Times* almost every day. Unfortunately, he is reading my *New York Times,* and some days he just tears out what he wants for his scrapbook, but other days he takes the whole paper home to read by the pool.

I was wondering if you could give Prince a calendar and then I will leave a day-old paper out every night in the hopes that he will take yesterday's paper every day instead of today's. This way he will be only one day behind in his news, but that will still give him a leg up on the other dogs in the neighborhood.

Sincerely yours,
   Ed

Dear Mr. Moran,

   Since retrieving your letter, my master has been hounding me to cease my morning strolls in your neighborhood, and I hope that you appreciate the fact that your *New York Times*es are no longer dog-eared. Obviously, all your news is not fit for Prince!

Your best friend,
   Prince

Author Teresa Bloomingdale believes that you do not even have to commit your letter to paper to get the beneficial effects. In *Life Is What Happens When You Are Making Other Plans*, she says, "Some people vent their spleen on the psychiatrist's couch, others at the dining-room table. I vent mine at the kitchen sink, where I compose scathing letters while scouring pots and pans."

When the principal asked that she write a note after her son was involved in a classroom scuffle, she thought about writing:

Dear Principal,

   My son tells me that he needs a note. This is a note.

Bloomingdale shares another letter she thought about sending to a bureaucratic banker:

Dear Mr. Friendly Banker,

If you're so friendly, why do you keep sending me nasty notes? I got your notice of my overdrawn account; you didn't have to follow it up with that mean letter. Here is your money, plus the penalty. How could the penalty be more than the amount of the overdraft?

Two other thoughts on exaggerated letter writing: After you write it, make sure you feel comfortable about sending it. If you do not, then send it directly to the wastebasket; you have probably already gotten the relief you needed just by writing it.

If you are actually going to mail it, you might want to indicate in the lower left-hand corner who will be receiving copies. List the president of the United States, members of Congress, the Pope, and the recipient's entire family.

One variant of exaggeration that makes fun of whatever bugs you is called parody. It imitates and often overstates the characteristics of another person or event. It is used by many comedians to get a laugh. Parody can also help you to laugh at your own stressful situations.

Imagine the following scene: Your son or daughter has gone off to camp for the summer. You have written twice a week for the past three weeks but there has been no reply. What kind of letter might you write making fun of this situation? Author Bennett Cerf suggests the following parody:

Darling,

Our home is fine. The food is okay and I like my wife. Yesterday we went on a trip to the golf course. The pro is nice and let me ride in a golf cart. I fed it some gasoline. Can I have a golf cart when you get home?

Today we had a competition downtown to see who could make money the fastest. I came in last. But your mother won the spending contest. Please send me a CARE package.

Love,
   Dad

Another form of parody you can use to lighten potentially difficult moments is to pretend you are some other person. (Do, however, be careful with this kind of parody; sometimes it can be offensive. Make sure that if you use it in company with others, they know that you are not putting anyone down, only trying to lighten things up.)

With this in mind, you might make believe that you are a Jewish mother and treat a problem by complaining, worrying, and suffering, or by making other people feel guilty. When the car runs out of gas, complain: "What, already you forgot, I put gas in the car three months ago." Even though you are only two blocks from home, worry: "What if we run out of gas again? How am I going to get home?" Suffer: "Don't worry. If we run out of gas, it's my fault." When the car does run out of gas again, make others feel guilty: "I'm not complaining, but who was the idiot that forgot to put gas in the tank?"

It does not matter that you are not Jewish, not a mother, or, for that matter, not even female. Anyone can pretend he is a J.M. The next time something upsets you, try it and watch your predicament become lighter. Cartoonist S. Gross has depicted a delightful J.M. scenario. It shows a Jewish mother standing on the street corner collecting money for her cause in a tin cup. The sign around her neck reads MY CHILDREN NEVER CALL ME.

By getting in someone else's shoes you see your problem in a new light. Try a parody of a Valley Girl ("Like, what a bummer, no gas. I can't believe this is *happening* to me. It's totally awesome. Like, wow. It's like so bunk"). Or maybe pretend you are Pee-wee Herman or a three-year-old child. Then you can see the car as an animated object and have a conversation with it, or imagine it (at least until you get some gas) flying through the air like Pee-wee's bicycle.

Tina Tessina, a therapist from California and author of *Love Styles: How to Celebrate Your Differences*, says that as soon as her husband sees an argument coming on between them, he heads it off by parodying a child. "Arguments are hard to have with a lovable three-year-old, which is what my husband can become at the drop of an accusation. He puts his hands on his hips, sticks out his chin, and (in a perfect imitation of a kid mimicking an angry parent) says, 'Who did that?' He then points his finger at whatever offense (a messy table, a forgotten chore) I've lost my sense of humor about. Watching him, I can't hang on to my anger. After we laugh, then we can do something constructive about the problem."

Household chores often become feel-like-crying situations if you detest doing them. Lynn Grasberg, a humor workshop leader, said that when her partner was not doing his share of the household duties she would enlist him as a fellow playmate and go into her kids-playing-grownups mode. "Honey," she'd importune, all saccharine and whiny, "do you know that we have garbage? Really, honey, the bags fill up just like clockwork. You know, dear, they need to be taken out once in a while." When her partner wanted to remind her that she too might not be doing her share around the house, he would go into *his* kids-playing-grownups mode: "Honey, do you know we have dirty dishes on the table?" This role-playing eventually developed into a regular family joke. "Honey, do you know that plants die if not watered?" "Honey, do you know that toilets need scrubbing?" "Honey, do you know that dirt gets into the house?"

In a restaurant, I once overheard an Iowa nurseryman relate how he turned the tables on an annoying customer with parody. He said his office phone also rings through to his house, and generally he is not bothered by too many customers calling during nonbusiness hours. One time, however, was different. The phone rang at 5:00 A.M. When he picked it up, the caller said, "I'm digging the holes for the trees you sold me the other day. How deep should the holes be?" He answered the customer and went back to sleep. At 5:00 A.M. the next day the phone rang again. It was the same farmer. "I forgot to ask you yesterday how far apart to plant the trees." The nurseryman answered and then went back to sleep. The third day the phone rang again at 5:00 A.M. "I forgot to ask how far apart the rows should be." "Spruce, eight feet. Elm, twelve," replied the nurseryman and again went back to sleep.

That night the nurseryman called the customer at 11:00 P.M. The farmer's telephone must have rung twenty or thirty times. Finally the farmer answered. "You the one who called me this morning, yesterday, and the day before at 5:00 A.M.?" the nurseryman inquired. "I just want to know how it's going." The farmer replied, "Do you know it's 11:00 P.M.? I thought everyone is sleeping at this time." The nurseryman replied, "That's funny. I thought everyone was up at 11:00 P.M. and sleeping at 5:00 A.M.!"

Psychotherapist Harold Greenwald uses a form of parody he refers to as a mirroring technique in which he impersonates his clients. You might want to try this kind of parody (with caution, of course) with someone who does things that annoy you. In *Humor and Psychotherapy*, author Thomas Kuhlman reports how Greenwald used this technique with a rather serious career woman who found it difficult to communicate with him.

> Trying to find the causes of this difficulty, I encouraged her to speak more about how she talked to her parents; she told me that as a young child she often found the only way she could speak to her father was if she was under the table in the dining room.
>
> "Why don't you get under the desk?" I asked her.
>
> "Oh, I couldn't do that," she answered with a giggle. "Why don't you?" she challenged.
>
> Happily, I perched under my large desk for the rest of the session; she spoke with much greater ease. At the next session when she hesitated I started to get under the desk again and she stopped me, saying, "Okay, okay, I'll talk— just don't go under that damn desk again." Then she added thoughtfully, "I guess I've been afraid to make a fool of myself by saying something silly or stupid. But since you showed me that you don't mind making a fool of yourself, why should I?"

Parody can also take the form of imitating and exaggerating procedures or events rather than people. Stressful work situations, for example, are ideal for this kind of humor. I am not talking about parodying your boss; this could get you fired. Instead, jokingly exaggerate office communication. For example, replace the complaint form with one that reads PLEASE WRITE YOUR COMPLAINT IN THE HANDY SPACE PROVIDED BELOW. PRINT LEGIBLY. and provide a miniscule space for same. Or mount the following notice near any piece of machinery that keeps malfunctioning:

WARNING
MACHINE SUBJECT TO BREAKDOWNS

> This machine is equipped with a "critical detector" that senses how desperate the operator is to use it. The detector

then creates a malfunction proportional to the operator's need. Threatening the machine with violence only aggravates the situation. Likewise, attempts to use another machine may cause it to malfunction too, since they belong to the same union. Say nice things to the machine and keep cool. Nothing else seems to work.

Or circulate this official executive pass-the-buck slip around the office:

TO:

READ AND: ____ Return
____ Retain
____ Route

ACTION: ____ Translate into English
____ Read & Weep
____ Read & Destroy
____ Destroy While Reading
____ Destroy Before Reading
____ Read & Pass On
____ Read & Pass Out
____ Read & Summarize
____ None of the Above

LEARN-TO-LAUGH EXERCISE

This exercise will help you exaggerate your feelings until— one hopes—they become so absurd that you begin to laugh.

Have a bad day.

If you are already having a bad day, then *really* have one. Complain endlessly about how rotten your day is, how uncooperative everyone is, how nasty your boss is (not to mention dumb, ugly, and stingy).

Pretend you are in the Oh-What-an-Awful-Day Olympics

and that you desperately want to win a gold medal. Jump up and down, throw a temper tantrum, crawl on the floor, and cry like a baby.

Warning: Use discretion as to where you do this exercise. It might be inappropriate on your nightly bus-ride home.

Laugh While the Irony Is Hot

Since no one knows quite how to measure irony, it is difficult to establish a recommended daily amount, but I think it is safe to say that no day is complete without a good dose or two of irony.

Joseph Meeker, *Minding the Earth* newsletter

Isadora Duncan, the great dancer, once suggested to George Bernard Shaw that they should have a child together: "It could inherit my beauty and your brains," she wrote to him.

Shaw demurred and wrote back: "Madam, I am flattered—but suppose it turned out to have my beauty and your brains?"

Life does not always give us what we plan for. In fact, sometimes you get the complete opposite of what you might expect. That is called irony.

You have probably experienced some absurdities in your life that can be classified as ironic—you get a raise, then come home to find your rent has been increased; you find the ideal job, then two weeks later the company closes down unexpectedly; the double-scoop ice cream cone you have been craving all day suddenly slips out of your hand and winds up decorating your brand-new shoes. Comical or horrible? Laughable or ludicrous? Comic irony or a terrible situation? The choice is yours. The world supplies the irony; you supply the adjective that describes it.

Intrinsically, irony is neither sad nor funny. What makes it *comic* irony is when we wind up somewhere so far from where we thought we would get that it is laughable. The key to turning just plain irony into comic irony is in seeing the absurdity in the relationship between these two elements.

O. Henry's famous short story *The Gift of the Magi* is a good example of irony. In this classic tale, a man sells his watch to buy his wife a set of fancy combs for Christmas, while she sells her hair to buy him a watch chain.

O. Henry's tale or the firehouse burning down may not be something to laugh about immediately, but seeing a bit of the absurd in these events makes for bittersweet comedy.

The comic in comic irony is not always immediately evident. Sometimes it takes a while to see that there is indeed some humor in discovering that what you wound up with is not exactly what you intended. A cartoon, for example, shows one unhappy man poring over the plans of a canoe looking for a clue as to what could have possibly gone wrong. In the background we see the canoe he just built—the front end pointing up, the back end pointing down.

One woman saw how the best-laid plans can easily turn into an ironic comedy. One Christmas she found just the right gift for everyone on her list. She realized, however, that her busy schedule would not allow her time to wrap them, so she had the department stores do it all for her. She took pride in finishing ahead of schedule, only to discover on Christmas Eve that none of the gifts had name tags. It seemed like a tragedy, until people began opening their tagless gifts. Suddenly everyone was laughing as her eighteen-year-old brother opened the box containing the sexy silk nightgown and her grandmother got the football shoulder pads.

I remember my Aunt Jessie creating some ironic comedy on her way to the doctor's office. She was told to bring in a urine sample for testing. She searched the house for a small bottle to put it in, but all she could locate was a perfume bottle, so she used that. When she got to the doctor's office the nurse wanted the specimen, but my aunt could not find it in her shopping bag. She realized that it had fallen out onto the subway car seat. She was upset with herself for losing the urine sample, but laughter eased her loss as she realized that somewhere in New York City some young man might be giving his sweetie a bottle of what he believed was expensive Chanel No. 5.

One man in the military spoke of the irony he encountered when he was assigned a new duty post. The government would pay for moving his belongings but not his aluminum rowboat. To get around the regulation, the officer filled the boat with dirt and rows of marigolds. When the movers came, he handed them a list of his possessions, which included "one oversized aluminum planter."

The popularization of computers is providing fertile ground for an entire new world of ironic events. When the computer is down you cannot get paid and when you get paid you cannot deposit it because the computer is down. I recently overheard one irate customer complain because the clerk could not sell her an item she desperately wanted. It seems that there were five of them left on the shelf, but the computer repeatedly refused the sale because it said that they were out of stock. Conversely, a publisher told me that according to the computer, they had 1,100 copies of a book remaining but could not find one to sell me.

The news media is constantly reporting ironic incidents that are either tragic or funny, depending on your point of view. Here are some that were chronicled within a twelve-month period:

- A Florida school board distributed fliers to fight illiteracy, urging everyone to "overcome literacy."
- A man in California won $9 million in the lottery because he forgot his wedding anniversary and played the wrong number.

- Some of the biggest sellers in bookstores were cookbooks and diet books; one tells you how to prepare food and the other how not to eat it.
- A plane designed to provide a safe, airborne command post for the president in case of a nuclear war was disabled after it flew into a flock of geese.
- An airline lost a man's luggage; nothing new or funny about that, except that he was the only passenger on the plane.
- The National Planning Association was not sure where their next year's convention will be.

Bo Lozoff, the director of the Human Kindness Foundation, which teaches prisoners meditation, says that "whether life's ironies strike you as funny or not depends on your sense of humor. I didn't laugh much when I was an angry radical in the sixties. And when I was a naive New Age seeker in the early seventies, I was never sure what was okay or not okay to laugh at. . . . Now that I'm not so angry or frightened, not only do I laugh a lot, but it turns out I have much more political and spiritual influence than I ever did in those joyless years when I was trying so hard. Ain't that a hoot?"

Lozoff points out that

God's best jokes are all around us. . . . Look at the great sums of money curly-haired people spend to straighten their hair, while straight-haired people are spending their bucks on perms. . . . Or the millions of dollars being spent so the Pope can visit the poor . . . And how come scientists never discover that soybeans or alfalfa sprouts are bad for us; it's always got to be something like ice cream or chocolate or booze or pot. . . . We're crazy as loons, struggling for illusions we can never get, on a planet that just doesn't support the style of life we try so hard to create. As the great cartoonist Gahan Wilson once said, "Life essentially doesn't work. And that's the basis of endless humor."

Seeing humor in things that do not work is another way of finding the comic irony of life. One down-and-out man realized this when he received a money order for fifty dollars, and the only person who could verify his identity so that he could cash it was someone to whom he owed forty-nine.

Playwright Gore Vidal reports that when his play *The Best Man* was being cast back in 1959, an actor named Ronald Reagan was suggested to play the leading role of a distinguished front-running presidential candidate. Reagan, however, was not given the part. Those casting the show felt that he lacked the "presidential look."

Several other celebrities have also had their day with comic irony. Fred Astaire's Hollywood screen test, for example, stated, "Can't act. Slightly bald. Can dance a little." And Charlie Chaplin once entered a Charlie Chaplin look-alike contest in Monte Carlo. The judges awarded him third place.

What we can learn from these stories, if we do not already know it, is that the world is absurd. There is not much we can do about that fact. What might help and what we can do, however, is to step back and find the comic in the absurd.

The *Washington Post*, for example, once ran a story about actress Mary Martin. She was walking down the Champs-Elysées in Paris one day wearing a stunning designer outfit. Suddenly a bird flew overhead, and before she knew it she was covered with droppings. Without batting an eye, Martin turned to her companion and said, "For some people they sing."

LEARN-TO-LAUGH EXERCISE

To find irony, you need to look at the relationship of how something started out and how it wound up. For example, one woman went to the head of a line of students registering for classes and loudy proclaimed, "I want to ask a question." (No irony here.) The registrar asked her to wait, but the woman persisted, "But I don't want to wait in line for nothing." (Still no irony.) Finally, the registrar stopped for a minute to handle the woman's question. "What time does the course start and who's teaching it?" the woman demanded. "What course?" asked the registrar. "Assertiveness training," replied the woman. (Ah ha!)

As a preliminary step to finding the ironies in your life, look for what I call "nutty news" in today's newspaper. Then, as you go through your day, stop from time to time and see if you can find some incident in which the relationship of what was intended and what resulted created some irony. See if you are able to see any absurdity in that relationship and if you can laugh (or at least chuckle) about it.

Attitude: Whistle a Happy Tune

Attitude is everything. Mae West lived into her eighties believing she was twenty, and it never occurred to her that her arithmetic was lousy.

Soundings magazine

Back in the Middle Ages, according to a story told by educator Edward Pulling, a dispatcher went out to determine how laborers felt about their work. He went to a building site in France.

He approached the first worker and asked, "What are you doing?"

"What are you, blind?" the worker snapped back. "I'm cutting these impossible boulders with primitive tools and putting them together the way the boss tells me. I'm sweating under this blazing sun, it's backbreaking work, and it's boring me to death!"

The dispatcher quickly backed off and retreated to a second worker. He asked the same question: "What are you doing?"

The worker replied, "I'm shaping these boulders into usable forms, which are then assembled according to the architect's plans. It's hard work and sometimes it gets repetitive, but I earn five francs a week and that supports the wife and kids. It's a job. Could be worse."

Somewhat encouraged, the dispatcher went on to a third worker. "And what are you doing?" he asked.

"Why, can't you see?" said the worker as he lifted his arm to the sky. "I'm building a cathedral!"

Have you ever noticed how some people are always "singing the blues," while others, no matter what they are doing or whatever happens to them, manage to "whistle a happy tune"?

It may seem as if we have no choice in the song we sing during life's painful moments, but we do. Although we may not have control over *what* happens to us, we do have a choice in *how* we see it.

When I lived in New York City I would walk my dog every day and meet an elderly woman walking hers. She would tell me all about the murders, robberies, rapes, and fires within a three-block radius (and it being New York, she had lots to tell). I nicknamed her the Voice of Doom.

I do not know why, but it took me months to realize that I did not have to listen to the Voice of Doom. I could cross over to the other side of the street and walk my dog in the opposite direction.

All of us have that choice. We may not be able to physically cross to a new street, but we can always walk down a different street by changing our attitude.

The following anonymously written poem is in five parts. Each one represents an attitude. Which chapter best fits you?

An Autobiography in Five Chapters

Chapter 1

I walk down the street.
There is a deep hole in the sidewalk.
I fall in.
I am lost . . . I am helpless.
It isn't my fault.
It takes forever to find a way out.

Chapter 2

I walk down the same street.
There is a deep hole in the sidewalk.
I pretend I don't see it.
I fall in, again.
I can't believe I am in this same place.
But it isn't my fault.
It still takes a long time to get out.

Chapter 3

I walk down the same street.
There is a deep hole in the sidewalk.
I see it is there.
I fall in . . . it's a habit . . . but my eyes are open.
I know where I am.
It is my fault.
I get out immediately.

Chapter 4

I walk down the same street.
There is a deep hole in the sidewalk.
I walk around it.

Chapter 5

I walk down a different street.

Which way you choose to see anything depends on your attitude. Is it partially cloudy today or partially sunny? Do 50 percent of all marriages end in divorce or are 50 percent successful? Do rosebushes have thorns or do thornbushes have roses? Is the glass half empty, half full, or is the glass twice as big as it needs to be?

Playwright Oscar Wilde chose to see the glass as half full after witnessing a dismal production of one of his new plays. When asked by a friend, "How did your play go tonight?" Wilde replied, "Oh, the play was a great success, but the audience was a failure."

A friend, Marty Carls, refuses to buy anything unless it is discounted. He has such a passion for sales that, when it came time to make up an Indian name for him at a retreat we both attended, I christened him "Bargain Hunter." One day he told me about a great bargain he almost got. Someone on the street offered him some expensive video recorders in factory-sealed cartons at a hundred dollars each. How could he resist? Marty would take two.

The salesperson asked for the two hundred dollars and pointed down the alley to a warehouse where the merchandise could be picked up. Wanting to ensure that he was not being swindled, Marty insisted that he would give the guy only half the money and the rest at the loading dock. With the deal made, Marty drove around the corner to pick up his order. When he got to the warehouse, there was no man, no VCRs, and no one who knew anything about a street sale.

Marty had been taken, but to hear him tell the story he still got "a bargain." After all, he could have given the guy the full amount instead of only half; he did not lose a hundred dollars, he saved a hundred!

Every moment of your life you choose which pair of attitude glasses to wear. If you always wear dark ones, everything you see will be dismal. If you wear rose-tinted specs once in a while, things appear brighter. You can either cling to your circumstances and wallow in your suffering or you can alter your attitude and change your outlook. As the following story demonstrates, you determine whether you are in heaven or hell.

A fellow dies and finds himself being ushered into a huge, regal hall. There an enormous table is laid out with incredible delicacies. As he is being seated at the banquet table, someone comes from behind and straps a thin board along the back of each arm so that he cannot bend his elbows. He tries to partake in some of the wonderful delicacies but he cannot reach his mouth with his stretched-out arms. Looking around, he notices that the other people are also in the same predicament and are grunting and groaning at their condition.

The fellow gets up and goes to the being who first ushered him in. "This must be hell," he says, "but then tell me, what does heaven look like?" The being unstraps his arms and takes him across the hall. There he sees another huge banquet hall with another great table filled with wonderful foods. As he is getting ready to be seated, again someone comes from behind and straps boards to his arms; once more he cannot bend his arms to feed himself. Lamenting that this is the same unsatisfactory situation as before, he looks around to notice that the conditions are the same but the response in this hall is totally different.

Instead of wailing at their plight, all are contented as each feeds the one seated next to him.

A cartoon in the *Wall Street Journal* showed an unhappy woman looking at the total of her bill at the supermarket checkout counter. The clerk is saying to her, "Why don't you look at it this way: Prices are lower today than they ever will be." Our attitude colors whether we see prices higher today than yesterday or lower than they might be tomorrow.

A popular song of the 1940s, with lyrics by Johnny Mercer, advised, "You've got to ac-cent-tchu-ate the positive, e-lim-my-nate the negative, latch on to the af-firm-a-tive."

Being positive about the negative things that occur in your life is difficult, but it can be done.

One writer looked at the second reject slip he had received that day and declared, "I'm getting up in the world. This one is from a company that pays more than the first." In the same vein, a fisherman declared that things were getting better. Yesterday he went for four hours without catching anything and today he got the same results in merely three.

Conversely, many of us know people who are always negative. Take one grumpy husband, for example. Nothing his wife did ever made him happy. If she served him orange juice in the morning, he wanted prunes. If the toast was buttered, he wanted it plain. If the eggs were fried, he wanted them poached.

One morning, in an effort to get her husband to stop complaining, his wife cleverly fried one egg and poached the other. Then she waited for his response.

Looking at the plate, her husband grumbled, "You fried the wrong one."

Most of us are not quite as contradictory as this man, but many times we get so caught up focusing on the negative that we forget the positive. Millions, for example, immerse themselves in the newspaper each morning while riding to work. They begin their day by reading about the world's tragic events. Frequently they end their day in the same way, listening to the TV reports of troubled happenings. Of course it is important to know what is going on in the world and work to correct injustices, but it is detrimental to our well-being to dwell on these disasters if they depress us or prevent us from accomplishing our tasks.

In a world that continually puts emphasis on unpleasant happenings, we need to remind ourselves daily that there are joyous things in the world too. Even in negative times, there is always something positive. One man told me that although he might not like someone, he always tries to find one thing he can praise—"Gee, I really like your left earring today." Another woman said she begins her week with an attitude-adjustment exercise. She starts her Mondays off by giving a gift to the person who irritated her the most the week before.

In their book *Stress Breakers*, authors Helene Lerner and Roberta Elins suggest a technique called "White Lighting" to help parents remain positive during child/parent encounters. It can also be useful in any person-to-person conflict.

> As your most (and least) favorite young person enters the room, before you read the little darling the riot act for (a) the missing car keys, (b) the parking ticket, (c) the fridge door left standing open, (d) the pile of wet towels in the bathroom, and (e) the mangled state of your makeup stick, which you need to color over the circles under your eyes and which your teen borrows routinely to camouflage zits— stop and consider.
>
> Before you recite this standard list of adolescent wrongs, imagine a white light, an aura, around your child. Then name all the things you love best—his impish grin, her glorious smile, the innocent years, the close and comfortable times. Feel the tension begin to subside, absorbed into the wonderful white light. Now you can address your grievances in a calm and rational manner.

To help you focus on the positive, keep a "joy journal," listing the gifts that come into your life each day. You can write down tangible items that you either find, like some coins on the street, and items that people give you, like a balloon in a supermarket; or nontangible items, like unexpected smiles from strangers, rainbows and sunsets, or something that tickles your funny bone.

Or you might want to list twenty-five items that bring you amusement and pleasure. They can involve people, places, or things, as well as activities engaged in by yourself or with others. A few of mine would include walking on the beach, being with my daughter, playing Chinese checkers, and taking a bubble bath. In composing your own list, try and keep any costs involved with your activities under ten dollars; amusement does not need to be expensive.

When you are finished with your fun-things-to-do list, keep it in a prominent place at home or in the office and go *do* some of them.

Research on outstanding achievers shows that they use certain techniques to help them focus on the positive. I believe that these same tools can not only help us produce tangible results, like obtaining higher athletic scores or landing larger business accounts, but also help to provide humor support when we are attempting to add more laughter to our lives and losses.

These positive reinforcing techniques include treasure mapping, affirmations, and visualization.

Treasure mapping is actually creating a representation of what you want to happen. It is like putting your dreams on paper. If you want a new relationship in your life, for example, draw a picture of what your ideal person looks like and list all of the characteristics you like about that person and all that you dislike. Create them as vividly as you can, put them on paper, and keep this where you can see it regularly.

You can do the same thing if you want more laughter in your life. Surround yourself with pictures and other items that keep reminding you of your goal. My bulletin board, for example, is filled with cutouts of laughing lips, smile buttons, and clown cards. These little reminders are like road maps constantly showing me which direction I want to travel toward. When I get stuck in an upset and forget that it is laughter I am after, these pictures help me get back on course.

Treasure mapping has always helped me achieve my goals. Years ago, when I lived in New York City, I drew fanciful Victorian houses, wishing that one day I would own one; today I do. And currently in that house, above my desk, are several best-seller lists, with my book, *The Healing Power of Humor*, in the number-one position. It is my way of treasure mapping what I want to happen.

The second attitude-changer is affirmations. It is the assertion that something is true, whether or not it has actually happened yet. In *Think and Grow Rich*, Napoleon Hill wrote, "Whatever the mind of man can conceive and believe, he can achieve." You can achieve more laughter in your life, but first you have to affirm and believe that it will happen—not *might* happen, but *will*: *I find some humor in every situation. I see every upset as an opportunity. I can laugh again.*

The third attitude-altering technique is visualization. This is vividly seeing within your mind the desired end result of what you want to achieve. No matter what is happening to you, you can always close your eyes and visualize what you want.

I believe that we go in the direction of what we dwell on. I have therefore included the following story as a caution to keep your mental pictures, your visualizations, positive.

My parents live on the East Coast and I on the West. Since my father refuses to get on an airplane, the only way for them to visit me is either by car, bus, or train. Years ago, they decided to take the train across the country to see me. My father worried constantly that their checked luggage would get lost. He inquired about it when he made the reservations, again when he bought the tickets, and he called several times before departure to confirm that nothing would happen. At the train, he double-checked with the porter and once more in transit. And then, finally, when they reached their final destination, there was no luggage. It had never been transferred from one train to the other.

Keeping a positive attitude does not guarantee things will turn out exactly the way you want them to. Had my father kept things positive and not constantly worried about his luggage, it still might have gotten lost but he would have had a more pleasant trip.

The classic story about two brothers, an incurable optimist and a diehard pessimist, illustrates how to remain positive while facing the negative. When asked what they wanted for Christmas, both brothers had the same reply. Each of them wanted a pony. Christmas morning came and both ran excitedly out to the barn. They flung open the doors but found nothing in the barn except an enormous pile of manure. Disappointed, the pessimistic brother ran back to the house in tears. The optimistic one, on the other hand, picked up a shovel, started to dig, and declared, "With this much manure there must be a pony in here somewhere."

LEARN-TO-LAUGH EXERCISE

The long-running musical *The Fantasticks* has a song in it that begins: "Plant a radish, get a radish, not a brussels sprout."

Treasure maps, affirmations, and visualizations help you plant the right seeds when you want to change your attitude and learn to laugh at life's adversities.

TREASURE MAP

(This is an actual picture of what you want the results of your planting to look like.)

First, either draw a picture or secure a photo of yourself in which you are laughing.

Then, keep this picture in a place where you see it often. It is a reminder that you can laugh.

AFFIRMATION

(This is the water and the sunshine to help your seeds grow.)

You can either make up your own affirmation or use one of those below. Remember to keep it in a positive form and to repeat it to yourself as many times a day as you can; also write it on numerous three-by-five-inch cards and put them around your home, office, and car so that you continually see what you are trying to achieve.

Here are a couple of suggestions:

"I [fill in your name] will get one more bit of laughter in my life today."

"I [fill in your name] am thankful for the joyous things in my life."

Or trying putting this one above every mirror in your house: "This person is not to be taken seriously!"

VISUALIZATION

(This is your mental picture that the seeds can grow, mature, and bear fruit.)

The following exercise is best done in a quiet, comfortable place. Turn the telephone answering machine on and put the kids on hold. Either have someone read the following to you or tape record it and play it back whenever you want. It should be read slowly, pausing when it seems appropriate.

Allow your eyes to close. Take a few slow, deep breaths. Silently repeat the word *relax* to yourself with each exhalation. Feel your body softening. Feel your muscles going limp. Gradually allow your breath to settle to its own pace until it becomes as if the air is breathing you instead of you breathing the air. With each breath, fall deeper and deeper into a calm, rested state. Relax more and more with each breath.

Focus on your breath. Imagine it entering a tube that is connected to a large, inflatable clown. With each exhalation your clown gets bigger and bigger. Now, take a closer look at your clown. Notice how large it is. Notice its colors . . . the makeup. What gender is it? Is it wearing a hat? Does your clown have a name? What is your clown's most interesting feature? Take time to get a clear picture of your clown. (Pause)

Now focus on your breath again.

With each breath you take, your clown keeps getting bigger and bigger and bigger. Imagine your clown getting as large as the balloons in the Macy's Thanksgiving Day Parade . . . even bigger.

Your clown is always with you to help you lighten up your problems. Remember: Nothing, no problem, is too big for this gigantic clown.

In a moment, your clown is going to give you some advice on how to lighten up a problem or difficulty you are having. Do not judge your clown's answer. It may not be what you thought your clown would say, but just accept the answer. Just listen.

Okay. Ask your clown how you can see some humor in what appears to be a humorless situation. Listen for the answer now. (Pause)

When you have an answer, thank the clown for listening to your problem and showing you how to lighten it up.

Thank yourself for participating in this process and know that whenever you need a lighthearted solution, whenever you are feeling stressed, whenever you feel lost for an answer, just ask your clown. It is as close to you as your breath. All you need to do to contact your clown is to breathe into it.

Now, when you are ready, say good-bye to your clown and bring your focus to your breath again. Let it settle to a quiet, even pace.

Become aware of the surfaces around you. Where you are seated . . . the floor . . . where your legs are . . . where your arms are resting. And now, with each new breath, start to become more and more awake, more and more alert.

And now, take three deep, energizing breaths and open your eyes on the last one. One: Alert! Two: Refreshed! And three: Awake!

Reminders: Prop Power

A New York City bus driver has a shrunken head hanging over the coin box on his bus. When passengers ask why, he answers, "They wouldn't move to the rear."

A great deal of the way we feel is influenced by what we see around us. A restaurant, for example, with rich wood paneling, velvet-covered chairs, and Oriental rugs can make us feel warm and comfortable. On the other hand, one with garish, mismatched tablecloths, stained walls, and a broken tiled floor can be uninviting.

Since our surroundings play such an important part in the way we feel, and in either uplifting our spirits or in bringing them down, I cannot overemphasize the use of humor reminders, humorous decorations, and amusing props to help you steer yourself in a lighter direction.

A number of years ago, a team of behavioral scientists at King Alfred's College in Winchester, England, documented the importance of surrounding yourself with items that uplift. They designed, built, and tested a "humor environment" that contained a wide variety of amusing and entertaining items for the visitors' amusement. A mock-up spaceship, submarine, toilet, theater, and a central area contained displays of jokes and cartoons and masks and costumes for the participants' use, as well as toys and other gizmos and gadgets for people to play with for either their individual enjoyment or for social interaction.

Visitors were given standard psychological tests before

they entered the environment and then were encouraged to take part in any activity they liked once inside. Unbeknownst to the participants, while they were occupied with the paraphernalia in the various rooms they were also being observed through one-way mirrors. Standard psychological tests were given to them again upon leaving.

The results of the experiment revealed that the spirits of those who took part were elevated. Humor centers, which might include humorous props and other laugh reminders, therefore, concluded the research team, might be of value because they could enhance social harmony.

One of the present-day inconveniences that seems to cause a great deal of disharmony is traffic jams; our expressways have become daily distressways. You might curse and shout in traffic jams, but that gets you—both mentally and physically—nowhere. What might be more productive is if you carry a humorous prop in your car to help you accept what is happening and have some fun with it.

I always keep a jar of bubbles in my car. When I'm in a traffic jam, I roll down the window and blow some bubbles. People may think Lawrence Welk has come along for the ride, but that does not bother me. I am relieving my stress, and from the smiles on the faces of the people in the other cars, I can see that it is helping them, too. (Two women have told me that they do not even need a prop to help ease their anxiety in traffic jams. One simply mouths the words *I love you* and throws kisses to other drivers. The other looks in her rearview mirror and makes funny faces at herself.)

Traffic jams, whether on an actual highway, in your office, at home, or anywhere on the road of life, are all places where you can test your sense of humor.

You might want to carry with you, keep in your car, or stash in your desk draw something—some prop, some gimmick—that can remind you to make light of any troubling situation. A pair of Groucho glasses or a rubber chicken strategically placed might be just what you need to grab in order to save not only the day but also your sanity.

Your prop or gimmick probably will not make your "traffic jam" go away, but it will make things more pleasurable until you get through the bottleneck. You may not like where you are at the moment, but a bit of playful interaction with your prop can help you see your disturbance in a positive way.

To show people how quickly a single humorous prop can start to diffuse difficulties, I give each person in my audience a bright-red clown nose. What continually amazes me is how this small object can make such a big difference in people's lives.

After one presentation, Gail Golomb, a mother of two, wrote to say that she had been at a loss as to how to get her kids started in the mornings. Most mornings they were in horrible moods and difficult to awake. She reported:

> I reached for the red clown nose and put it on. I went over to a sleepy Gary on the sofa to ask him if he was able to finish all his homework while I was out during the previous evening. He mumbled a few answers, avoiding looking at me . . . and when he did, that kid got the biggest smile on his face! It was worth it just to see a smile prior to breakfast.
>
> Now Jennifer was another story. Still wearing the clown nose, I walked to her bed, expecting yet another struggle to wake up this child. I noticed her eyes were half opened, and I could tell by the expression on her face that I was in for a real story as to why she couldn't wake up. But you should have seen her eyes open in amazement, and she couldn't stop laughing! It was the best antidote to the Sandman I've ever seen.

Knowing my passion for red noses, Lola Gillebaard, a woman from Southern California, sent me a newspaper clipping entitled "The Key to a Successful 30-Year Romance Is a Red Nose." It mentioned the workshops on relationships that Lola and her husband, Hank, lead in which they teach people how to use a clown nose to head off arguments. They suggest that partners make a deal: If one of them gets angry, that person puts on the nose. The idea is to keep conversation to a minimum until things cool down. "When I get angry," Lola says, "I put on a large red nose and that tells Hank that he'd better not try to talk to me right then." She adds, "I forget I have it on, and when I see myself in the mirror, I laugh. Sometimes that makes it hard to stay angry."

Wearing clown noses may work around the house, with office mates, or with friends, but it may not be as appropriate in other situations. Dr. Bill Plautz of San Francisco General Hospital has figured out a way to solve this dilemma. He carries a rubber Cyrano de Bergerac nose in his pocket. When upset with someone, he gets relief by putting his hand in his pocket and playing with it. He can thumb his nose at his opponents, turn it up, or even pick it, and no one is the wiser.

Funny signs are another kind of handy prop to have around your work space or in your home. They can be straightforward ones that help you remember to laugh, like IF YOU ARE TOO BUSY TO LAUGH, YOU ARE TOO BUSY, or STAMP OUT SERIOUSNESS, or ARE WE HAVING FUN YET? Or they can be laugh-producing signs that actually get you to laugh, like NEVER WRESTLE WITH A PIG. YOU BOTH GET DIRTY AND THE PIG LIKES IT, or WE DO PRECISION GUESS-WORK! or even EAT A TOAD FIRST THING IN THE MORNING. NOTHING WORSE CAN HAPPEN TO YOU FOR THE REST OF THE DAY.

Funny signs can also help you get your message across so that people will remember it. For example, one restaurant that did not cash checks posted this sign: WE HAVE AN AGREE-MENT WITH THE BANK. WE DON'T CASH CHECKS. AND THEY DON'T SERVE PASTRAMI SANDWICHES. Another res-taurant, which was having trouble with people putting their cigarettes out in the coffee cups, put this sign on the wall: IF YOU MUST PUT CIGARETTE ASHES IN THE CUP, TELL THE WAITER, SO HE CAN SERVE YOUR COFFEE IN THE ASHTRAY."

Props are great to help you put upsets in reverse, but what about those moments when you are propless? Do not worry. The world is full of them. Anything can become a distress-relieving prop. Objects like a telephone, a spoon, or a handkerchief can quickly be called into action to help you lighten up.

I have been known to grab a parking meter, for example, and use it as a microphone to state my case to my disagreeing companion. When a little levity is needed to relieve boring dinner conversation, I use the dinner napkin as my prop. I drape it over my face, put my glasses back on over the napkin, and continue eating dinner that way.

One person told me that he uses his telephone as a toy. When things get too hectic in the office, he either pretends that he is Alexander Graham Bell answering a newfangled machine, or responds in a foreign accent, or makes believe he is Lily Tomlin and speaks in an Ernestine-the-operator voice ("One ringy-dingy, two ringy-dingys . . .").

A woman in one of my workshops related this account of how an ordinary teaspoon came to her rescue. She and most of the secretarial staff would have lunch together on a regular basis. She partially enjoyed these times because all participants had an informal agreement not to discuss work-related issues. But there was one exception: A woman named Janice always managed to disrupt the peaceful break by complaining and whining about her boss.

Yes, Janice's boss was disagreeable and inconsiderate, and they all empathized with her, but they simply did not want to hear about him at lunch. Asking her to stop complaining had no effect, until one of the secretaries came up with the following idea: As soon as Janice began with her audible sigh, she put one hand up to stop her, grabbed a teaspoon with the other, and, using it as a microphone, announced: "We interrupt this broadcast with a special newsbreak. We have Janice Bloss here, secretary to the infamous J.J. Stuffed Shirt, with details of his outrageous behavior. Ms. Bloss, please speak into the microphone and tell our audience of J.J.'s most recent accomplishment in the name of pseudo-efficiency and compulsive disruptions."

With encouragement from the "interviewer," Janice began to complain about J.J.'s latest tirade. But she could not keep her whining monologue up—indeed, she could not stop both blushing and laughing. Janice even surprised us by taking a spoon back to the office. Whenever J.J. got to her she would come over to one us, hand us the "microphone" and ask to be interviewed. Sometimes just showing the spoon was enough to elicit anything from smiles to fall-down laughter.

What is delightful about using a humorous prop is that you do not need to be quick-witted, memorize a joke, or even know how to tell one. Just let the funny item do most of the work.

I once demonstrated the effectiveness of "prop power" at a hotel luncheon. I was warned that I might not want to sit at a certain table. When I asked why, I was told that the table had a very intimidating waitress. "She is big, burly, and most unpleasant." Sensing that a humorous prop could save the day here, I waited until the waitress finished serving the first course and then handed her one of the foot-long hundred-dollar bills that I use in my workshops. "You're doing such a great job today that I want to give you something," I said. "I'll bet this is the largest tip you have ever received." Her face lit up. "Well, honey," she said, "it may not be the largest tip, but it sure is the biggest bill." She laughed, we laughed, and as she returned to the kitchen one woman at the table remarked, "Look she's even walking differently now."

Another example of prop power: A young man nicknamed his father Godzilla, so frightened and overwhelmed was he by him. One day he was asked to role-play and confront his "monster" father in a psychotherapy session. He sat there frozen. He could not say a word until the therapist suggested that they call in a consultant to help get over this impasse. The therapist got up, opened the door, and brought in a six-foot-tall inflatable Godzilla. After the laughter died down, the young man started to talk freely once he realized that his fear of his father was as inflated as the toy Godzilla.

A number of people like the therapist above are using toys to ease tense situations. San Francisco's Moffitt Hospital, for example, makes use of puppets to explain to young patients what kind of operation they will be having; the facts become less scary than when presented by a doctor or a nurse.

Another difficult situation in which puppets are being employed is with molested children; what children are too frightened to retell they may be able to act out with puppets.

Toys, like puppets and stuffed animals, are not just for children. Several hospitals are now using Sir Koff-a-lot bears with adult patients who have undergone open-heart surgery. These people need to cough after the operation, and the hospitals are finding that the patient is more apt to do it when hugging the bear than they are with the traditional blanket or pillow.

Major corporations too are hiring the Muppets to explain such potentially upsetting events as reorganization changes, salary freezes, and employee cost-cutting drives. Kermit the Frog even helped TV newscaster Ted Koppel explain the Black Monday stock market crash. The puppet lightened up the disheartening news without playing down the seriousness of the situation.

Gail Wenos, a professional ventriloquist, thinks puppets are great in feel-like-crying situations because they give you license to vent your feelings and say things you might be afraid to otherwise utter. Wenos uses Ezra, her "smart dummy," to do this. "By the time I'm finished," she says, "or by the time Ezra has had his say, I'm feeling better, the other person has gotten the message but isn't offended, and the air is cleared."

Puppets are not the only less-stress toys you can use. Workers in one office keep a soft plastic toy hammer that makes a funny squeaking sound when it hits something. When the computers do not work properly they yell out, "I need help with the computer. Where's the hammer?"

Senator Charles Grassley, a Republican from Iowa, uses a toy to relieve his Capitol Hill stress. Grassley has a briefcase marked TOP SECRET that contains an electric train set complete with track, miniature animals, a small farmhouse, and an engineer's cap. When things get out of hand in his office, he puts on the hat and starts the train. Grassley's press secretary says, "It makes me laugh just to think about it. The senator zooms the train along the track—and suddenly the mood around the office has lightened."

If you are not the engineer type, or if your boss is not an Amtrak fan, you may want to consider other kinds of humorous props. Photos of yourself or others with funny expressions are great for this. Go to a photo booth and have one of those strips of photos taken of yourself with four of the most outrageous faces you can make. Then keep this handy for when you are overly solemn.

When I am lecturing, I always carry a picture of my daughter Sarah that was taken when she had a pie thrown in her face. If things are not going well I simply glance at the photo, and I am soon revived by the expression on her face.

Photos became an important part of a team-building effort for one woman who was in my class. She said that after she had been made the manager of her department, people started seeing her as superior and not communicating with her. She solved this feeling of separation by asking people to bring in baby pictures of themselves. She put them on the bulletin board, and everyone tried to guess who was who. After a week, she said the baby-picture guessing game humanized and changed the relationship between her and the department.

LEARN-TO-LAUGH EXERCISE

Toy stores, garage sales, and secondhand stores are great places for locating inexpensive laugh reminders.

As you go through your day today, look around you and notice which items bring you joy and which bring you down. Replace those that upset with some that uplift.

Let a Smile Be Your Umbrella

A smile is a curve that sets everything straight.
                                    Phyllis Diller

Smiles is the longest, shortest, and quickest word in the English language.

You probably know why it is the longest—because there is a mile between the first and last letter. It is also the shortest, because a smile is an instant communicator, and the quickest, because a smile is the swiftest way to get rid of your doldrums.

On the surface, the simple act of turning up the corners of your mouth provides an instant connection between you and someone else. There are no language barriers when you are smiling. That smile on your face is a light to tell people that your heart is at home.

On a deeper level, when you are smiling you are also triggering less-serious memories within your body. According to a study done by psychologist James Laird of Clark University, facial expressions can trigger our moods by returning us to happier memories. Laird found that students remembered happier thoughts when they were smiling; conversely, grim stories were more easily remembered when they were frowning. In other words, if you are anxious asking for a raise, making a business call, or even telling a joke, try smiling; it can help you recall a time when things went well.

"It now seems clear," says social psychologist Fritz Strack of West Germany, "that facial expressions are an integral part of emotional experiences." Strack, who conducted similar research to Laird's, found that his subjects' reactions to cartoons were enhanced when he forced them to smile by having them hold a pen in their mouth.

Both these researchers agree that it does not matter if you are smiling for real or faking it. A phony smile can trigger happy thoughts just as easily as a genuine one. "So if you really want to appreciate humor," notes Strack, "it's important that you smile—even if you have to fake it a bit."

As with the investigation of laughter, the medical world is beginning to validate the benefits of using your zygomaticus major muscles—or smiling, as it is commonly called. Smiling, according to Dr. David Bresler, can help us take the first half-step away from our physical and psychological pain. It is only a part of an overall picture, but when we can smile in spite of our pain, we begin to focus away from our discomforts.

In early childhood development, a smile precedes a laugh. Babies smile within the very first week after birth; laughter is not evident until about the third or fourth month. Bresler, a former director of the pain control unit at the University of California in Los Angeles, therefore, starts with the predecessor to a laugh, a smile, and encourages his patients to move away from their pain by smiling. He even writes prescriptions for his patients that direct them to go to the mirror and smile twice an hour.

Bresler also encourages patients to increase their smiling by expanding their "serum fun levels." "People with chronic pain," he says, "often don't do things they would normally enjoy. They feel they can't because of the pain. But it's often the other way around. Their pain actually persists longer because they don't have any fun."

Many years ago, Gelett Burgess, the man who wrote the "I never saw a purple cow" poem, went to a lecture in Paris that changed his life. The speaker had started his presentation by asking everyone to laugh. Burgess had been going through a troubled period in his life and had not laughed or smiled for some time. But that evening he could not help it. The simple suggestion, compounded by the fact that everyone else was laughing, brought a smile to his face. Before he knew it, he was feeling better.

The next day he cut a picture of a smiling face out of a magazine and pinned it on the wall. Every time he looked at it, it made him smile too.

He began collecting pictures of people laughing and smiling. Soon he had a scrapbook full. One day he showed it to a nurse, who in turn passed it around the hospital. People felt better just looking at the smiling faces.

Burgess continued to make other scrapbooks and sent them to his ailing and depressed friends. The reports he got back were always the same. Everyone felt better.

Dr. John Diamond believes that smiling, or even looking at a smile, as Burgess did, gives us what he calls "life energy." "We have always known," says Diamond, "how beautiful and beneficial a smile is. Now we can show—actually demonstrate—the therapeutic value of smiling." In his book *Your Body Doesn't Lie*, he states that smiling helps strengthen the thymus gland, an important contributor to a healthy immune system, because the zygomaticus major (those smile muscles) and the thymus gland are closely linked.

Reports of the advantages of smiling have come from both the scientific and nonscientific fronts. *USA Today*, for example, suggested that to ease Christmastime pressures you smile as widely as you can and then repeat the process several times. Of course, it does not have to be Christmas to smile. Stop reading and smile for a count of ten. Then relax your facial muscles for another count of ten. Repeat this funny-face exercise once or twice more until you can feel the tensions ease.

Yvonne Rand, a Zen priest, uses a half-smile technique to get a perspective on her anxieties. "Mouth yoga," as she calls it, consists of lifting the corners of your mouth slightly (not a full smile or a grin, but only a half smile) for a space of three breaths. In an article, published in *The Windbell*, Rand wrote about her half-smile practice. She notes:

> When I first began doing the half-smile, I did it whenever I found myself waiting. So I did it whenever I came to a stop sign or a stoplight. I did it standing in line at the checkout stand in the grocery store. I did it when I was on hold on the telephone. I did it when I was waiting for an appointment in the doctor's office or waiting for someone coming to see me. . . .
>
> What I found was that in doing the practice whenever I was waiting, that after a while, after a month or so, it also occurred to me to do the practice when I noticed some feeling of anxiety or anger arising. . . .
>
> Most of all, I find that the half-smile is practice that brings me to some sense of spaciousness, and in that spaciousness I notice more than I do when I am feeling crowded by my pace, or my activity, or by the expectations I hold for myself in terms of what I want to get done this morning, or today, or this week—or maybe even in this lifetime.

Rand is not the only one who has found power in a smile. Waitresses say it pays to smile; they report making bigger tips when they do. In hospitals, patients felt that a smiling nurse helped them heal quicker than a nonsmiling one. And finally, thieves who held up 7-Eleven stores divulged that they did not rob clerks who greeted them with a smile.

And smiling, like laughter, is contagious. If you do not believe me, just look at the face of Alfred E. Neuman in *Mad* magazine. Chances are, if you know this drawing, you are already smiling just thinking of it.

Many songs have been written to remind us to smile— "Pack Up Your Troubles in an Old Kit-Bag and Smile, Smile, Smile," "When You're Smiling," and "Smile, Darn You,

Smile" are but a few. My favorite smile song is a little-known one from the Broadway show *Annie*, "You're Never Fully Dressed without a Smile." The lyrics remind us that it is not what you wear from head to toe that counts, but what you wear from ear to ear.

Smiling, even faking it, can help lift you up when you are down by not only raising your energy but also by connecting you to others. "A smile," it has been said, "costs nothing, but gives much. It enriches those who receive, without making poorer those who give. It takes but a moment, but the memory of it sometimes last forever."

It has also been said that "If you can smile when all else is going wrong, you must be a plumber working for triple time on a Sunday."

LEARN-TO-LAUGH EXERCISE

If indeed faking a smile is as beneficial as doing it for real, then go ahead and do it. Smile. How do you feel when you are smiling?

Now, frown and notice how you are feeling.

Okay. Now go back to your normal face, whatever that is.

Maybe you noticed that it felt better to smile than not to. And perhaps you will do it more often.

If you are still having trouble smiling, try what Virginia Tooper does. She has a six-inch cardboard cutout smile with an elastic band on it. When she does not feel like smiling, she puts it on. Then she looks in the mirror. Suddenly a real smile happens under the cardboard one.

Child's Play: Making Molehills
out of Mountains

Children have a remarkable talent for not taking the adult world with the kind of respect we are so confident it ought to be given. To the irritation of authority figures of all sorts, children expend considerable energy in "clowning around." They refuse to appreciate the gravity of our monumental concerns, while we forget that if we were to become more like children our concerns might not be so monumental.

Conrad Hyers, *Comic Vision and the Christian Faith*

"One evening," writes Richard Lewis in the magazine *Parabola*,

I went out to have dinner at a Japanese restaurant. I sat near two children, about six or seven years old. Amidst the refinement of a beautifully set table, the voices of these children were about to alter the mood of the setting:

First Child: 'Why did the girl blush when she opened the refrigerator door?'

Second Child: 'Because she saw the salad dressing.'

Grins, a burst of giggles, and a warm laugh from everyone within hearing—and the world, for the moment, had somehow righted itself again.

Children are an important source for righting ourselves when we feel like crying. Children have a unique way of looking at the world. Their perspective can teach adults an important lesson: Burdens can become less weighty when we use our imaginations to play with our problems.

Our imaginations are wonderful tools for turning our troubles around. We can use our childlike imagination to play with any unpleasant occurrence or turn any task into a game.

To a child, everything is a game. The world is a huge playground. Play is a vital element in a child's development. When we are growing up, we learn about the subtleties and complexities of our surroundings through play. As adults, we lose sight of the fact that play, be it mental or physical, can once more help us deal with our world. It can change our energy, provide relief from our problems, and even help us find solutions to them.

Making a game out of a difficult task or situation turns it into play. The world, and everything in it, therefore, becomes an adult playground too.

Dr. O. Carl Simonton, co-author of *Getting Well Again*, says that "play is essential for life. . . . It is not selective, it is mandatory." Simonton is so convinced of the value of play that he teaches juggling to cancer patients. He says that play takes our mind away from our problems. If you think about your illness—or any other difficulty, for that matter—while juggling, you will drop the ball.

In my workshops I get people moving around the room doing things like jumping up and down, shouting out the last digit of their phone number, and making the letter "H" with their bodies. There is often much laughter and a sense of renewed vitality in the room after these exercises. The games illustrate how quickly play changes our energy. By playing around with those things that annoy us and turning them into a game, we change the energy we have toward our upsets, we free our creativity, and we help solve our problems.

Cheryl Thorn, a mother of three, said that she frequently saw her children use games to turn their upsets around. When her oldest daughter was four, Cheryl noticed that whenever one particular friend came over to play there were never any fights. So one day she asked her daughter, "Iyan, how come when Adam comes over you two never fight?" Iyan replied, "Adam showed me a game to play whenever we start to argue. We put our hands together and push against each other. It makes us laugh, so we never fight."

Cheryl's two other children have also shown her how to counteract upsets and fears with play. When Mariana, her youngest, was learning to ride a bicycle, she frequently fell. One day Cheryl noticed Julian come over, put his arms around Mariana, and shake her. Then both of them vigorously stamped their feet on the ground. Julian informed Cheryl that they were shaking and stamping out Mariana's scared feelings.

Dr. Simonton emphasizes the need for physical play. I believe that mental play is mandatory too. Instead of logically trying to figure out the solution to a problem—and often getting stuck when no solution seems feasible—allowing ourselves to mentally play in our imagination can often lead to a solution.

Adults forget that the creative child's mind is still within us and that, like a child, we can use our imagination to change our perception of the things that annoy us and to give a new perspective to our problems.

Children use their imagination to become whomever they want to be and to transport themselves to wherever they want to go. You too can do the same thing to help pick you up when you are down. By playing in your mind, you can uncreate what you do not like and recreate what you want.

Imagine yourself in a job in which you deal with the public throughout the day. Suddenly an irate person comes over and starts yelling at you. One way to keep your perspective and not get involved in the ranting and raving is to use your imagination and mentally play with the situation. A receptionist in a probation office relates that when incidents like this occur to her—and they often do—she uses some mental play. She thinks of people as animal types. "They might come to me as grizzly bears, but I soften them by seeing them as teddy bears."

Sometimes mind play can lead to actual humorous solutions to our problems and help make molehills out of mountains. One homemaker, for example, used her imagination to counteract her husband's constant complaints about getting the same thing for lunch every day. He opened his lunch box one day to discover that his wife had filled it with a coconut and a hammer.

Some people have used their playful imaginations to turn annoyances into games. One woman said she makes a game of her work. She sets quotas for herself and then tries to surpass them. She gives herself a gold star for each sale she makes; for every ten she gets, she sends herself a bouquet of flowers.

Seminar leader Jim Pelley turns parking his car into a game. He says that when he gets frustrated trying to find a space, "I imagine that there is one and only one available, and it is my goal to find it."

William Daniels, a college professor from Schenectady, New York, made a game out of getting his students to show up for their finals. Over a period of years, he had his exams either delivered by helicopter, embedded in a chunk of ice, or baked in cookies.

One man made a game out of what to do with his garbage during a New York City sanitation department strike: He wrapped his garbage each night in some fancy gift paper and left it on the front seat of his unlocked car. By morning it was gone.

If you have trouble understanding how playful thinking can lead to problem-solving, try glancing at some of the stories that people share in *Reader's Digest* each month.

For example, a Chicago physician received some unsolicited ties in the mail. Accompanying the ties was this letter:

"We are taking the liberty of sending you these exceptionally fine ties. Because these ties have the approval of thousands of discriminating dressers, we know you will like them. Please send twenty dollars."

The indignant doctor replied: "I am taking the liberty of sending you twenty dollars' worth of extra-fine pills. These pills have helped thousands, and I am sure you will appreciate my thoughtfulness in sending them. Please accept them in payment of the ties that you sent me recently."

In another instance, one customs inspector who works at the highway border wrote that he often got sore throats because he tried to outshout the noise of cars, radios, fans, and so on. Now he simply mouths the first question. Motorists have to turn off their radios and engines, roll down the window, and ask him to repeat himself.

If you are still having trouble seeing how you can solve your problem with some humorous play, think about how your favorite comedian might do it. How would Lucille Ball, the Three Stooges or Groucho Marx handle your crisis?

The above comedians might throw a pie in the face of someone annoying them. And while you do not have to go to such extremes, you can certainly use some mind play to imagine, say, a fellow worker who constantly nags you wearing a pink-and-green punk-rock hairdo, dressed in a tutu, standing in his underwear, or sitting on the john. This last image is particularly appropriate with your superiors; it takes them off their pedestal and puts them on the throne.

A childlike view of the world can frequently put adult life in perspective. In a small book entitled *Don't Cross Your Bridge Before . . .*, first-grade schoolteacher Judith Frost Stark gives us a glimpse of the way children often think.

A penny saved . . . is not much.

Opportunity only knocks when . . . she can't reach the doorbell.

When the cat's away . . . no pooh!

Comedian Dom DeLuise gives us another example of a child's unencumbered view of the world. He says that there was a time when nothing made him laugh. "Everything was wrong—life was hopeless and I was feeling useless." When his son asked what he wanted for Christmas, DeLuise replied, "Happiness—and you can't give it to me." On Christmas day his son handed him a piece of cardboard with HAPPINESS written on it. "You see Dad," he son said, "I can give you happiness!"

It is this unique perspective that often causes adults to laugh at what children say. It is also this innocent view of the world that can help adults to not be so weighed down by their problems.

Gary Deluhery, director of a day-care center, relates the following story of how a child's perspective helped him turn a mountain back into a molehill. It was the center's annual multicultural dinner, created as a chance for parents, children, and staff to celebrate both their diversity and their ability to work well together. The previous year's celebration had been quite difficult for Gary, as he had just been hired as the new director. This year, he planned things out early so that he could relax and participate in the dinner—or so he thought.

At first just minor things went wrong. Then someone dropped the slide projector that was to be used for an after-dinner presentation. When the dinner itself was over, the woman who had been hired to take the children to another place to play did not show up. The kids became restless and began running about. In the midst of all this commotion, an elderly woman insisted on someone moving the car that was blocking hers in the parking lot. With his tension—and temperature—rising, Gary went to help her navigate out of the lot. Just as he started back into the building, one of the young children came charging down the stairs and threw herself at him.

The images that flashed across Gary's mind as the child was flying through the air included an injured child, shocked parents, and people saying, "You see, he cannot control or even protect our children!" However, as he instinctively reached out his arms, he not only caught her but also caught her laughter and exhilaration. Immediately, those first terrible images melted away. Swinging her around, the child's enthusiasm reminded him that this was a *celebration.* Her laughter and play did not fix things, but it did change Gary's perspective. And the evening continued better for him and for those around him.

In *The Joy of Working*, authors Denis Waitley and Reni Witt suggest that we go through our day as if we were doing everything for the first time, like a child might. "When faced with a routine—typing letters, answering the telephone, selling door-to-door, filling out forms—approach each task as if it were your first time. . . . The same applies to a sales presentation. Even if you've pitched the product a thousand times before, it is the first time for your customer. Make it fresh and interesting."

This first-timer's view of the world makes everything an adventure for a child. Life can be filled with adventures if adults want to look at it with the playful eyes of a child, or it can be replete with misfortunes if we choose to see life with overserious eyes.

Ann, a woman in one of my workshops, told me how her young son helped her get a new perspective on her upsets. She was having one setback after another: She recently separated from her husband; her place of business closed; her car conked out. Just when she thought she could not handle one more thing, her water heater exploded. No significant damage, but a horrible mess. As she was about to begin the major cleanup, her young son burst into the room, saw what happened, and exclaimed, "Oh, good, we're having another adventure!"

Even as adults, we can tap into our inner child's sense of

adventure and unique way of seeing the world. We were all children once, and some part of us still is. Some part within is still wanting to say the things we are not supposed to say, wanting to run through the halls of the library, or take off our shoes and play in the sandbox. And while many of the things children get away with are inappropriate for adults, children can still teach us much about freeing ourselves from our burdens. Whether it is using our imaginations to alter our upsets or actually adding some play element to our painful situations, ten seconds of child's play is sometimes all it takes to shift our focus from the dark moments to the lighter ones.

LEARN-TO-LAUGH EXERCISE

The Zen teachings have a concept similar to the openness of a child's mind. It is called "beginner's mind." "In the beginner's mind," it is said, "there are many possibilities; in the expert's, there are few." The exercise that follows can help you look at a problem with a childlike beginner's mind. It combines all of the elements just discussed: play, games, and imagination.

When facing something that seems insurmountable, gather some friends and present your problem. Then, as if this were a child's game, have them randomly call out solutions that come to mind, whether or not they make any logical sense.

For this to be a beginner's-mind session, however, certain rules must be followed. Answers should be short and without much forethought; none can be questioned; and all solutions, no matter how silly or absurd, are considered. In fact, funny ideas and silliness are encouraged.

When I was having a terrible time finding anecdotes for this book, several friends and I had one such session. These were some of the solutions we came up with:

- Have a come-tell-me-your-story table set up at a busy downtown intersection.
- Start a story-collecting telephone chain—have ten people call ten others.
- Run classified ads.
- Wear a button that says "I'M WRITING A BOOK—TELL ME ABOUT IT."
- Tap Herb Caen's telephone.
- Hire a story writer.
- Ask a librarian.
- Have a slumber party.
- Talk to kids.
- Ask taxi drivers.

Sorting through the ideas, some made me laugh, some seemed too farfetched to actually use, some opened up pathways for other ideas, and some I actually went and used. The process itself was most valuable because, even if no concrete ideas had come out of the session, it got my juices flowing and opened my mind up, like a beginner, to all sorts of possibilities.

One last thought on this process: Because it is such a fast one, tape record it.

Add Some Nonsense

A little craziness once in a while prevents permanent brain damage.

Adults often tell children, "Grow up." Perhaps one of the wisest things adults can do is to "grow down"—to do or say something from time to time, as children frequently do, that makes little or no sense.

One of the meanings *Webster's New World Dictionary* gives for nonsense is "things of relatively no importance or value." This may be an accurate description of nonsense itself, but when used in conjunction with feel-like-crying situations, nonsense can be of great value and importance in helping us escape our dilemmas.

In researching this book, I asked a number of professional humorists for tips on how they add levity to difficult situations. A couple of responders (whose stories follow) talked about seeing the absurdity of things and suggested that one way to accomplish this was to do something nonsensical. Like a jump-cut scene in a movie, a little bit of nonsense introduced into our problem instantly switches the picture on us and changes the focus.

Art Fettig, a funny man from Michigan, recalled this battlefront story illustrating how a dash of nonsense helped him get through a highly volatile situation:

I was a combat rifleman in Korea with the First Cavalry Division. I had a friend named Fred Bolt who was just as crazy as I. Each morning, just to keep our sanity, or else to demonstrate our insanity, Fred and I would jump out of our respective foxholes and sing the theme song from Don McNeal's old radio show "The Breakfast Club." It went, "Good morning, breakfast clubbers, good morning to you. We woke up bright and early just to how-de-do-you. Here's Fred and Art, that's just the start . . . we bid you all adieu. 'The Breakfast Club' is on the air!!" Then Fred or I would break out into a hearty song. We never got through our song because every morning the Chinese would start bombarding us with mortars, and we would leap back into our holes for cover. Somehow this bit of nonsense got us through an impossible situation. In November, both of us were wounded and we both survived the war. I truly believe that our sense of humor got us through.

Today, on the home front, humorist Hope Mihalap relies on nonsensical accents to turn when-you-feel-like-crying situations into laughter:

When someone in my household does something that annoys another, nine times out of ten the irritated person will issue a reprimand in some insane and inappropriate accent. This makes both the offender and the offended person laugh—and points up the fact that the situation wasn't all that darned serious after all. Example: If my husband forgets that I've had a hard day and have only just finished cleaning up the kitchen after a huge, complicated dinner and foolishly says, "Honey, now would be a good time for you to make all the bag lunches for school tomorrow," I can either burst into tears and snap, "Don't you realize I've been in the kitchen long enough?" Or—and this is what I usually do—I can begin singing the "Song of the Volga Boatmen" and stagger hunchbacked across the room before responding, "Vot you tink I yam, a *slave*?"

This sort of thing will inevitably get the right responses:

(1) laughter; (2) a good-natured apology; or (3) help. And if I'm lucky, all of the above.

Nonsense is also an effective tool in the office, providing that you have both established a rapport with your fellow workers and your boss and your timing is appropriate. Since you will want to avoid getting fired, explore the following trio of ideas with caution:

- When things get really bad at work, start a "Light Opera Day" and sing to each other for a minute or two.
- On a sheet of toilet paper, list the names of all the people who have angered you in the past week. Then at the end of the week, flush it down the john.
- Make a list of all the curse words you want to use. Give each a number. Next time something upsets you, pick three numbers and shout them out.

This last suggestion is similar to one used by a minister. Whenever he would encounter a painful experience, like breaking a dish or stubbing his toe, he would shout out, "Grand Coulee!" When asked what he meant by "Grand Coulee," the minister replied, "Grand Coulee—why, that's the world's largest dam, isn't it?"

Often our days become frustratingly boring because we do the same thing over and over again. We drive to work the same way, perform the same job, lunch with the same people, even eat the same kind of sandwich. Naturally, we are disappointed because our life is dull. Do something different; a bit of nonsense thrown in our daily routine from time to time helps spark it up.

Tomorrow, try starting your day by getting out of bed on the other side. Eat your breakfast with the opposite hand. Take the elevator to either one floor above or one below the one you are going to and then walk up or down one flight. Walk up a hill backward. Pay the bridge toll for the person behind you. Dial a prayer and argue with it. Tell everyone it's your birthday when it is not.

Need something nonsensical to do? At the dinner table tonight? At your office tomorrow morning? Try reading the following paragraph, from Neil Anderson's *The Ha Ha Book*, aloud:

> HA HEE HEE HEE, HA HO HA! HA HO HO HO HEE HO HEE HO HEE HO HA. HA HO HEE HEE HA HA HO HA HEE HO HA. HA HO HEE HEE HEE HEE, HA HO HO HO HA HO HO. HA HEE HO HO!

If you are really having a bad day at the office or at home and you need a physical stress-relieving nonsensical activity, try getting up and tap-dance. Sharon Peterson, a college administrator from California, says tap dancing is great in feel-like-crying situations, because "you can't tap-dance and be unhappy."

If you are not in the mood to imitate Fred Astaire, perhaps the following bit of nonsense will help. Adapted from *Playfair*, by Matt Weinstein and Joel Goodman, it not only gets everyone laughing but also gives you some support. So on those days when nothing seems to be going well, when the negatives outweigh the positives, when you need a little help from your friends, ask for a standing ovation. Next time you've burned the dinner, get up and shout out, "I've just burned the dinner, and I want a standing ovation!"

Authors Weinstein and Goodman say that this exercise frequently lingers on after they have shown it to people. "We often hear reports of students jumping up on a table in the cafeteria and bellowing out, 'I just finished my physics midterm and I want a standing ovation!' followed by a thunderous explosion of whistling, cheering, and table pounding by the assembled student body."

Moreover, once people get into the habit of asking for standing ovations whenever things are not going well, just mentioning those two words, *standing ovation*, without anyone even responding, often brings laughs and the needed moments of relief.

Another nonsense technique can be borrowed from the world of film and theater. Some plays or movies use what are known as "asides," when the actor steps out of character and talks directly to the audience.

Here is how an aside might work for you. Suppose your four-year-old comes into the living room and spills a bowl of cereal on the newly cleaned rug. You can step outside of yourself by turning to an imaginary audience and vent your upset: "Why couldn't he spill the cereal in your house? Maybe you'd like to take him home for a week. How about a few years? Why not forever?" Or you might say, "Mother told me there'd be days like this. So that's why Aunt Alice remained a spinster."

Asides can also work well in arguments, since it prevents you from getting caught up in the encounter. At the right moment, turn and ask your make-believe audience, "Did you hear what she said? Can you believe that? Tell her she's got to be kidding."

Another nonsense technique is similar to an exaggerated letter, but here you not only create the letter but are also the one who answers it. The mother whose son spilled the milk on the rug might write to him and then write a reply back from him. Or, better yet, she might do the same by going directly to the source: God.

Dear God,

How can you be so cruel? I spent the entire day cleaning the living room rug. Then, even before it was dry, four-year-old Ian came into the room and spilled a bowl of cereal and milk all over it.

Bernice

Dear Milk Maid,

Please forgive me. I was having a pretty dull day. Traffic was moving along without an accident, I forgot to create a whopping thunderstorm that the weatherman had predicted, and I was tired of making the Dow fall.

So, when I saw Ian coming into your wonderfully clean living room with an overflowing bowl of cereal, I knew I just had to create another Milky Way. I thought it was hilarious. Sorry you did not. What can I say? I could tell you not to cry over spilt milk, but that has been uttered before.

Love and kisses,
    God

P.S. Give Ian a big hug for me.

Actress Helen Hayes has a story of how her family used some nonsense to ease what could have been an uncomfortable situation. As she was preparing dinner she warned them, "This is the first turkey I've ever cooked. If it isn't right, I don't want anybody to say a word. We'll just get up from the table, without comment, and go down to the hotel for dinner." When she returned from the kitchen about five minutes later, all family members were seated at the dinner table— wearing their hats and coats.

Comedian Johnny Carson used some sophisticated nonsense when besieged by reporters after he was signed for *The Tonight Show.* He gave the reporters a list of ten answers and let them furnish the questions to suit. They follow: "(1) Yes, I did. (2) Not a bit of truth in that rumor. (3) Only twice in my life, both times on Saturday. (4) I can do either, but I prefer the first. (5) No. Kumquats. (6) I can't answer that question. (7) Toads and tarantulas. (8) Turkestan, Denmark, Chile, and the Komandorskie Islands. (9) As often as possible, but I'm not very good at it yet. I need much more practice. (10) It happened to some old friends of mine, and it's a story I'll never forget."

A couple of years ago, I saw nonsense help someone come out of depression. A friend from the East Coast was severely depressed after the loss of a loved one, so I invited him to come to San Francisco for a change of pace. During an outing to Monterey, we encountered the usual tourists taking pictures of the California coast. I did not bring a camera with me, but that did not stop us from taking pictures. I asked Bob to stand near some rocks by the ocean as I snapped away with my imaginary camera. As we were taking our make-believe photos, one woman, who wanted to cross in front of me, politely ducked to avoid being in the way of our picture taking. Her perplexed husband looked at me, then at Bob, but he could not locate a camera. Not wanting to take any chances, however, he too ducked down as he walked between us. Bob and I still laugh about this and manage to take some fake photos every time we see each other.

In *Humor: God's Gift*, pastor Tal Bonham talks about how some nonsense helped break the ice between his wife, who had been hospitalized for severe depression, and some of her friends. He writes:

Depression!
I secretly wondered if my wife would ever laugh again. . . .
As we drove home from the hospital that day she

looked into a mirror and exclaimed, "Yuk, I look like a witch!"

"A visit to the beauty shop will do wonders for you," I suggested. " But if you insist," I said, "I'll tell your friends when they call that you've emerged successfully from the hospital except for one problem."

"And what is that?" she asked.

"I'll tell them that you think you're a witch and that you ride a broomstick around the house!"

She laughed. "Why don't you?" she asked.

"Are you serious?"

"Yes, maybe it'll break the ice a little bit. People never seem to know just what to say to someone with emotional problems," she explained.

Later that evening, one of her friends called and asked if she and another friend might come over to see Faye.

"Come right on over," I said.

"Well, how is she?" asked her friend. "Are there any aftereffects?"

"Only one," I explained deliberately and compassionately. "You see, she recovered well from the treatments except for periodic spells when she thinks she's a witch."

"She thinks she's a witch!" her friend yelled into the phone.

"Yes, from time to time, she'll jump up, run to the kitchen, get the broom, and ride it across the room. It doesn't last long. I suggest, if she has a spell while you are here, that you just remain calm and act as though nothing is happening."

Later in the evening, Faye's friends came laden with gifts of perfume and, thankfully, much food. I could tell that it was difficult for Faye to talk about her stay in the hospital. Then, I noticed a gleam in her eye as she got up from the sofa in the den and walked to the kitchen.

She was going to do it!

Her friends were sitting with their backs to the kitchen, and I was facing them. As Faye mounted her broom, she smiled at me like a child about to take the lid off the cookie jar to steal a cookie.

"Giddy up!" she called as she rode the broom from the kitchen, made a *U* turn in the den in front of her friends, and galloped back to the refrigerator. Their eyes followed every stride as she deposited her faithful steed in the kitchen corner. They kept talking about something else, but their eyes and their minds were focused on Faye and her broom.

When she returned to the sofa, her friends were strangely silent and seemed to have nothing more to say. When we finally explained our little plan to break the ice, we all laughed boisterously and enjoyed a delightful evening of conversation thereafter.

Jean Westcott, a communication expert, recalled a time when she and two collegues were asked to design a logo for a department in a large company. Try as they might, none of their drawings worked. As their frustrations mounted, their creativity diminished. Then one of them got silly and started joking around by drawing an obscene version of the logo. The laughter that ensued released the tension and got their creative juices flowing again. They were then able to complete the job.

One nurse revealed how nonsense helped her cope after she gave a patient an enema but did not get any results. She waited for quite a while but the patient still produced nothing, so she gave him another. Again she waited, to no avail. Desperate, not knowing what to do, she picked up his T-shirt, assumed the attitude of a cheerleader, and shouted, S-H-I-T, S-H-I-T! The patient laughed so hard that the nurse finally got what she was after. Sometimes nonsense makes the most sense.

LEARN-TO-LAUGH EXERCISE

This exercise uses a little bit of nonsense to help you get a perspective on your problems.

Identify some difficulty, problem, or anxiety in your life. Start with some small irritation or loss.

Now state out loud whatever is bugging you ("My husband never puts his dirty clothes in the hamper," for example). Then immediately after, repeat one of the following phrases: "Ha, ha," "Ho, ho," or "Tee, hee." Try to say these last couple of words with lots of expression.

Putting the two together, it would look like this: "My husband never puts his dirty clothes in the hamper, *tee hee.*"

Do you feel silly stating your problem and then making fun of it?

That is just the point! When you can play with your problems—even if only in your imagination—you start to get a distance from them, you start to let them go.

(This idea was adapted from the work of Annette Goodheart, a laughter therapy specialist.)

Wordplay

"The question is," said Alice, "whether you can make words mean so many different things."

Lewis Carroll, *Alice Through the Looking-Glass*

It may seem elementary, but words are a major influence on our actions. One study found that when people were told that they had a good sense of humor, whether or not they actually did, they were so encouraged that they made many more attempts at saying or doing funny things than before they were praised.

In one of his books, author Vernon Howard speaks about a man who wrote down what he called beautiful words in a small notebook. They included such words as *joy*, *love*, *crystal*, *blossom*, *sparkle*. Every morning this man would read about a dozen or so words from his list. When the opportunity arose throughout the day, he would use them in conversation. He told a friend, "Because I looked at the world only through rose-colored words, I became rose-colored myself."

Read the following words very slowly to yourself:

unhappy	sullen
upset	dark
tears	morose
depressed	sad
gloom	dismal

hopeless	misery
bleak	somber
sorrow	despair

How do they make you feel?
Now read the following:

joyful	cheerful
mirthful	amusement
joking	merriment
giggle	delightful
happy	fun
laughter	jovial
glad	jolly
silly	hilarious

Does the second list make you feel any different than the first?

If, as many people believe, we are what we think, then maybe we need to rethink the things that disturb us and re-label them. Renaming your experiences can alter the way you view your upsets. The shift is slight, simply christening something with a new name, but the impact is often major, because it reframes the upset. Just as the frame of a picture affects how it looks, so too when you reframe your upsets they appear different. It is almost like receiving a package wrapped in torn and dirty newspaper as opposed to the same package beautifully wrapped in gold foil and ribbon. The contents are no different, but the packaging makes a vast difference.

If your TV is always breaking down, for example, you can steer into your upset or try and maneuver out of it. Renaming the TV "Old Fadeful" might help you chuckle about it instead of cry about it.

Working with someone who is unpleasant? Try giving him

a private nickname like "Cookie," "Pumpkin Pie," or "Rosebud." Tired of the constant complaints around the lunch table? Replace the SMOKING and NO SMOKING signs with BITCHING and NO BITCHING.

I went through many painful moments writing this book. One morning after completing a particularly difficult section, I accidentally pressed the wrong key on the computer and instantly erased everything I had just written. I was devastated by my loss, but I was determined to use laughter to ease my situation. For the next few weeks, I told everyone I met that I was no longer a writer. I was now an eraser.

One family used the renaming tactic to give away a litter of twelve puppies. First they put an ad in the paper that read: "Free to Good Home—Adorable Puppies." After several weeks most of the litter was still left, so they changed their tactic and ran another ad. This one read: "Free to Good Home—One Very Ugly Puppy and Eight Pretty Ones." Within two days, they had given the "ugly" puppy away nine times.

Joan, a hospital nurse, said she began to see her work in a less burdensome way after she used some wordplay to describe her job. At first she said her work was pretty depressing. It involved taking care of critically ill people until they get better and leave or die and leave. After rewriting her job description, she noted, "I'm a body scratcher, patcher, wire attacher, and bedpan snatcher."

For many people, the aging process is very upsetting. If you have not yet noticed, as you get older things start to either wear out, fall out, thin out, or spread out. Reframing with humor the fact that you are getting on in years can help ease that reality; you acknowledge the fact without getting overly concerned about it. George Burns constantly laughs about his years. "Eighty is a beautiful age. It takes very little to turn me on, and sometimes when I think I'm turned on, I find out I'm not even plugged in." Burns was once asked how it felt to be eighty-five years old. He replied, "When I feel eighty-five, I'll let you know."

Dorothy Duncan, a seventy-year-old friend, feels that much of the language associated with the aged is demeaning. She would like to see some of our aging-related words changed. As a firm believer in aliveness in aging, Dorothy has alerted her definition of retiring to "replacing the tires on my car." In addition, she does not consider herself a senior citizen; she says the phrase has no meaning to older people, because there are senior vice-presidents, senior tellers, and senior partners who are often in their twenties and thirties. Dorothy feels that a more fitting term for people who have gotten on in years would be "vintage persons." "VPs," she says, "can be any age and, like fine wine, get better each year."

One "vintage person" home uses rewording to reframe the capabilities of residents who need wheelchairs and walkers to get around as opposed to those who do not. In the cafeteria there are two signs. One reads CANE and the other, ABLE.

Literally interpreting what people say—or, in other words, taking things at their face value—is another wordplay technique that can help relieve our burdens. For example, one person said, "A wonderful thing happened this morning. A man knocked on the door, and when I asked who he was he replied, 'A bill collector.' So I gave him my stack of bills."

Most of us are not so naive as to misinterpret a bill collector's intentions, but still there is a good lesson here. Taking things literally can produce humor that literally saves the day.

For example, I get annoyed at telephone solicitations, but I have found an amusing way to cut them short. I give them exactly what they ask for. Usually they begin by wanting to know how I am, and do I have a minute. I answer, "I'm fine," and "Yes, I do." I then turn to the clock and time them. At the end of sixty seconds, if I am not interested in what they are selling, I interrupt their sales pitch, let them know that their one minute is up, and politely end the call.

Jean Westcott said that every time she went off to a meeting, her boss would insist that she leave a phone number in case of an office emergency. This was absurd, since her job involved long-term organizational planning; in the ten years she has been on the job, there has not been one emergency. Nevertheless, her supervisor asked her for a forwarding number every time she left her desk. Jean finally solved the problem by doing exactly what her boss requested. She left a number at which she might be reached. It was for Dial-a-Prayer.

In another case, the only way one man was able to reach a busy executive was by using some literal humor. When he asked to speak to Mr. Fischer, the secretary always screened the call and did not put him through. This time was different. When she said, "May I ask who is calling?" he replied, "Certainly, I'm the one who wants to speak to Mr. Fischer." The secretary connected him immediately.

For the most part, literal humor is safe humor. It gets your point across without offending. Arthur Godfrey, the television personality, used it one day to gently get a persistent fund-raiser off his back. When asked by the fund-raiser why he had ignored numerous letters inviting him to join one committee or another, Godfrey replied, "All your mail was on stationery that read 'From the desk of So-and-so.' I never correspond with furniture."

Actress Carol Channing did the same with an overly inquisitive fan. "Do you remember the most embarrassing moment you ever had?" asked the admirer. "Yes, I do," she replied. "Next question?"

Literal humor can occur on two levels. The first is when someone tells or asks you something and you unintentionally misinterpret it. This happens unconsciously; you usually see the amusement after the fact.

For example, one woman related how she went to the drive-up window of her bank on one particularly windy day.

Before she put her deposit through the window, the teller requested, "Please put the weight on your check." She could not understand why the teller asked her to do this, but she did as she was told and wrote "165 pounds" under her name. After she drove off, she laughed hysterically as she realized that the teller had not meant her body weight but rather the paperweight that had been provided to keep the checks from blowing away.

The other level of literal humor involves times when you deliberately misinterpret something. For instance, when a waitress routinely asks if there is anything else you would like, you could answer, "Yes, there is, now that you mention it. I would like a Jaguar, a new house, a winning lottery ticket." Here literal humor is used to create an amusing moment and perhaps establish rapport. But the real value of literal humor in feel-like-crying-situations is when it can be used to ease annoyances and stress.

Groucho Marx deliberately misinterpreted a letter from his banker to make light of business correspondence clichés, which he despised. The letter he received from his bank manager concluded with the line, "If I can be of any service to you, do not hesitate to call on me." Marx wrote back: "Dear Sir, The best thing you can do to be of service to me is to steal some money from the account of one of your richer clients and credit it to mine."

An older woman used literal humor to turn an annoyance into amusement. Because she still maintains such a youthful appearance in spite of her years, she is continually being asked her age. She then has to listen to their surprise and be told over and over how young she looks. She is tired of it. So now when asked her age she simply tells people—in Roman numerals. This year she will be LXXVI.

One last literal humor story involves an encounter between the poet T. S. Eliot and a young lad who was hoping to become a poet himself someday. In *Remembering Poets*, Donald Hall recalls asking Eliot for some advice. The poet obliged. "Forty years ago I went from Harvard to Oxford. Now you are going from Harvard to Oxford. What advice can I give?"

Eliot "paused delicately, shrewdly, while I waited with greed for the words I would repeat for the rest of my life, the advice from elder to younger, setting me on the road of emulation." Then, says Hall, "when he had ticked off the comedian's exact milliseconds of pause, he said, 'Have you any long underwear?' "

To increase your own literal humor skills, go to a greeting-card store. Notice how they use this kind of humor to turn simple statements around. For example, the outside of a card reads, "Since it is your birthday, I want to tell you how I feel." You open the card up and it says, "I feel fine, thank you."

Now go through your day and notice how you can turn overseriousness around by taking things literally.

LEARN-TO-LAUGH EXERCISE

This will help you rename and reframe some of your upsets.

Dr. Bob Basso, author of *Light Management*, suggests an exercise called "Draw Your Dragon." Using paper and crayons, he advises that you draw an outrageous cartoon of the person who gives you the most hassles. Then give the cartoon a silly name and look at it just before a conflict occurs.

Another related Basso technique I call "Name Your Monster." Find an inanimate object that irritates you and rename it with a fun name. One man who works with seven computers dressed them up with hats and scarfs and named them after the seven dwarfs. Sometimes he says they even act like their name—Dopey, Grumpy, Sleepy, and so on.

(You might also want to shroud your computer with a

black cloth when it is down, or, if it is not obeying your commands, treat it like a puppy in training: "Sit!" "Stay!" "Off!")

I've noticed that San Franciscans use a form of "Name Your Monster" with certain city buildings. St. Mary's Cathedral is frequently called a seventeen-story washing-machine agitator, and the former Jack Tar Hotel was known as the box that Disneyland came in.

Author Teresa Bloomingdale takes naming your monster one step further—she rates her "misery makers."

One star (*) goes to people who only occasionally frustrate her, like messy popcorn eaters who don't clean up after themselves; they probably can be forgiven, she says. If they do it regularly, then they become two stars (**), along with the casual caller and the hotel reveler; they, according to Bloomingdale, "should be forced to take an est course." The three-star jerks (***) "should be run out of town"; these include the theater talker, the manic driver, and the parking space grabber. Finally, the highest rating, four stars (****) goes to people like the bully and the reformer; Bloomingdale classifies them as goons. She advises, "Eliminate them."

Let Go

As two monks were walking down the road they noticed a young woman waiting to cross a stream. One of the monks, to the dismay of the other, went over to the woman, picked her up, and carried her across the water. About a mile down the road, the monk who was aghast at his friend's action remarked, "We are celibate, we are not supposed to even look at a woman, let alone pick one up and carry her across a stream. How could you possibly do that?" The monk replied, "I put that woman down a mile back. Are you still carrying her around with you?"

When we do not let go of our upsets, difficulties, and disappointments, they become burdens on our shoulders. Their weight prevents us from laughing. In order to get more levity in our life, we must stop struggling with our circumstances, let go, and accept what we have been given.

In his book *Laughter and Liberation*, psychologist Harvey Mindess says, "We must learn to accept. . . . To accept life and to accept ourselves, not blindly and not with conceit, but with a shrug and a smile. To accept in the end existence, not because it's just or reasonable or even satisfactory, but simply and plainly because it's all we've got."

"When the infant comes into the world," notes Dr. Wayne Dyer, "it has not thought that the world can or should be any different from what it is." As adults, however, we are constantly trying to change our surroundings. Then we get frustrated because we cannot. We can work for things in our life that we would like to see bettered, but as Dyer tells us, "the trick is to do it without getting angry at the world for having problems in it."

It is important to take a stand and work for the things we want to see changed. But when we get overly caught up in our efforts to fix things, to intervene, to make things better, we lose sight of life's larger picture and process.

Dr. Bernie Siegel, author of the popular book *Love, Medicine and Miracles*, advises us to let go when he says, "If you could live your life with a 'we'll see' attitude, it is amazing what begins to happen." In his talks, he illustrates this point with the following story:

> There is a man who has a farm, and his whole livelihood depends on his horse to plow the field. One day he is out plowing and suddenly the horse drops dead. The people of the town say, "That's very unfortunate." And the man says, "We'll see."
>
> A few days later somebody feels sorry for him and gives him a horse for a gift. The townspeople say, "You're a lucky man." And the man says, "We'll see."
>
> A couple of days later the horse runs away and everybody says, "You poor guy." And the man says, "We'll see."
>
> A few more days go by and the horse returns with a second horse, and everybody says, "What a lucky guy." And the man says, "We'll see."
>
> The man had never had two horses before, so he and his son decide to go riding, and the boy falls off one of the horses and breaks a leg. The townspeople say, "Poor kid." And the man says, "We'll see."
>
> The next day the militia comes into town grabbing young men for the army, but they leave the boy behind because he has a broken leg. Everybody says, "What a lucky kid." And the man says, "We'll see."

If we just wait a while—not jump into an argument, not draw conclusions too soon, not act immediately—many times our upsets decrease.

One father uses this technique to handle his children's nagging and complaining. If it is not an emergency, he has them write all of their annoyances on a "Saturday list." Then on Saturday morning he sits down with them and goes over their grievances. Nine out of ten times the things they were upset about have either been forgotten, cleared up, or are not so important anymore. "One of the great secrets known to internists but still hidden from the general public," says author/educator Lewis Thomas, "is that most things get better by themselves. Most things, in fact, are better by morning."

There is something to be said about allowing nature to take its course. I learned this lesson several years ago at a seven-day winter retreat I was managing. One hundred fifty people spent most of their time in a single-room rustic building. The room was heated, but those sitting near the windows or doors frequently complained about how cold it was; those in the middle of the room complained how hot it was. For the first day or two, I was constantly raising and lowering the thermostat or opening and closing the windows. It became so that no matter what I did, I could not please everyone. I finally decided to set the thermostat at one temperature and let the participants take care of themselves.

People would constantly bob up and down throughout the day, either opening or closing the window. Then as I watched, the situation humorously solved itself. One person pushed the window a bit too hard and it fell out into the creek below. The fact that the room was either too hot or too cold was never mentioned again for the rest of the retreat.

At a retreat my friend Henriette attended, the leader was a master at teaching the students about letting go. This was a ten-day meditation retreat where the entire day, from six in the morning to ten at night, alternated between forty-five minutes of sitting meditation and forty-five minutes of walking meditation. The only break from this routine was for meals, which were eaten in silent meditation, and the evening talks, which were given by the teacher.

Everyone in the meditation hall sat on either a small cushion or bench. Each day the students would return to the same floor space they had chosen at the beginning of the retreat. At about the sixth day, the teacher rearranged many of the cushions and benches while the students were at dinner. When they came back into the meditation room, there was chaos. Nearly everyone was upset because the spaces they had established for themselves had been changed. Here they were, spending hours trying to let go of their attachments, and in one split second the teacher showed them just how hard they were in fact hanging on.

I learned another lesson in letting go from my attempts at city gardening. Since I grew up in an urban environment, the thought of going to my own garden and picking what I planted excited me. Thus, one spring I worked for several days digging, planting, and watering. In the weeks that followed, I watched, but there was not much to see. Just as quickly as the seedlings came up, they were devoured by the snails. Each time I would plant, the snails had a feast. I tried seeds. I tried seedlings. I tried ash around the starts. I tried plates of imported beer to intoxicate the snails. I tried snail bait. Nothing worked. Nothing grew higher than a half inch. In desperation, I returned to my more predictable indoor environment and relieved my frustrations by writing the following:

Though snails are incredibly slow
There is one thing I'd like to know,
If I outrun 'em round the yard
How come they beat me to the chard?

Letting go of my green-thumb attempts actually paid off. I sold the poem to *Organic Gardening* and used the money to buy vegetables from the corner produce store.

In our effort to hold on to the way we think the world *should* be instead of seeing it as it is, we, like a horse with blinders, narrow our vision. In our nearsightedness, we resist change, we try to hold on to what we have lost, and we cannot see what the moment has to offer. If we want to ease our hurt, live fully, and be full of laughter, we must let go. "Part of the happiness of life," says Dr. Norman Vincent Peale, "consists not in fighting battles but in avoiding them. A masterly retreat is in itself a victory."

Letting go is a hard thing to do when things are not going well—for example, when you are angry at your boss for not granting you a raise, or you are upset at your children because they will not turn down the stereo. But often you get quicker results, with less effort, when you simply let go and do not get caught up in a situation. The louder we yell at the kids to turn down the stereo, for example, the more upset we become and the farther away we get from the peace and quiet we wanted in the first place.

When the children refuse to turn down the stereo, you might simply let go and allow them to play it as loud as they want while you use the time to coffee klatch at a neighbor's. Or, if you want to let go with humor, you might use some of the techniques suggested elsewhere in this section to relieve your frustrations. You might, for example, exaggerate the situation: Tell your kids that they are playing your favorite album; you would love to hear it at least ten more times and could they please turn *up* the volume. Try a bit of nonsense; mouth your request to turn down the stereo as if they have gone deaf. Remember prop power: Borrow a tuba from the school band and start your practice just when the stereo begins blaring. Or change your attitude; insist on dancing with them to the music of the Screaming Sex Pots (or whoever is blasting away).

Our upsets are like a car on an ice-slicked road; the more you try to steer away from the ice, the harder it is to do so. The trick to maneuvering in such conditions is to let go of where you want to go and turn into the skid. Or, as est founder Werner Erhard puts it, "It's much easier to ride the horse in the direction it is going."

In the October 1986 issue of *Reader's Digest*, Albert Vajda writes about trying to order an egg in an Italian hotel with only a very limited command of the native language. The lesson he learned was it is sometimes best to let go and just go with the flow; the added bonus he got was a good laugh:

> I tried first with the English "egg." No reaction. I told him in French *oeuf*, in German *ei*, in Latin *ovum*, and finally in my native Hungarian *tojas*. No success, no understanding, only an inquisitive look. How can I get an egg for breakfast? Suddenly I had an idea. Being a cartoonist, I took a piece of paper and drew an egg.
>
> The effect was surprising. *"Si, si,"* the waiter said happily. *"Patate!"* Which is the Italian for potato. I shook my head and quickly drew an egg cup under the egg.
>
> *"Si, si,"* the waiter said with a broad smile. *"Cognac."* With head and hands I waved "no" and made another drawing (of a chick hatching from an egg).
>
> *"Si, si,"* the waiter said enthusiastically. *"Pollo."* Which is the Italian word for chicken.
>
> At this point I gave up. I told him to bring me *colazione*, which is the Italian word for breakfast.
>
> Five minutes later he brought me coffee, butter, marmalade, rolls—and one three-minute egg. The regular breakfast for that hotel.

Letting go involves developing an attitude of noninterference so that you can step back and watch an event instead of getting involved and perhaps trapped in it. The late author/ critic H. L. Mencken did this masterfully and lightheartedly when responding to the controversial letters sent to him. He would simply answer: "Dear Sir (or Madam), You may be right!"

Sheila and Bill Bethel are both professional speakers and seminar leaders. One day Sheila came home from a week-long tour on which she had a series of particularly successful speaking engagements. For hours, she was so wrapped up in her triumphs that, even though she had not seen her husband for a week, she neglected to pay much attention to him. Rather than get upset, Bill let go of his expectations about Sheila being back in town. He allowed her to carry on about her success. Then, when she seemed finished, he asked with some gentle humor, "May I have my wife back now?"

Letting go is like one of those Chinese straw puzzles, the kind you stick an index finger into each end of and then try to pull out of. What happens is that the more you pull and the more you struggle, the more tightly you become trapped. The trick to the puzzle is to relax. When you let go and do not forcefully try to escape, your fingers slip out easily, and you are free.

LEARN-TO-LAUGH EXERCISE

In *The Sky's the Limit*, Dr. Wayne Dyer suggests that we write the upsets that we have little control over on a "forget-it list." The best we can do with these items, says Dyer, is to laugh them off, because "that's just the way the world turns."

This is a good idea for most of our upsets, but for those particularly difficult ones, the ones that give you Excedrin headache number 954, you may need a more powerful ritual.

I suggest you write these kinds of irritations on a piece of paper, tie it to a helium-filled balloon, and then release the whole thing.

He Who Laughs First

*When we admit our schnozzles, instead of defending them,
we begin to laugh, and the world laughs with us.*

Jimmy Durante

For centuries, the Jews have known that when you can laugh
at yourself or your situation, others will be more likely to
laugh *with* you and not *at* you. By learning to laugh at themselves and their predicaments, they have often become
the victor over their afflictions. You too can learn this same
lesson.

A word of caution before you begin: Laughing at yourself
or your situation is not the same thing as putting yourself
down. Putting yourself down can undermine your self-esteem
and make you and those around you uncomfortable. Laughing
at yourself allows you and others to acknowledge the situation
in a way that eases it and may even improve self-esteem and
respect.

After her dress came apart at a state function, Eleanor
Roosevelt turned to those around her and proclaimed, "There
seems sometimes to be a hopeless discrepancy between
me and my clothes!" If she had responded by swearing or
making a comment like, "Oh! What a fool I am for wearing such a dress," both she and the guests would have felt
uncomfortable. Instead, Roosevelt got the upper hand on her
embarrassing situation by being the first to poke fun
at it.

Virginia Tooper also tells a story about a time when a bit
of self-directed humor helped her steal her enemies' fire:

The hardest job I had was substitute teaching in junior high. An eighth-grade boy got mad at me over a math assignment I gave him and went all over school telling everyone that I was a centerfold in *Playboy* magazine. I was fuming mad. At recess, two regular teachers sidled up to me in the coffee room and wanted to know if what they heard . . . was, uh, true. All at once I found myself putting the pain in perspective as I responded, "It is a mean, nasty lie, and I certainly hope no one gets a hold of August of '61."

Actress Shirley MacLaine has used this same laugh-at-your-self-first kind of humor in order to quell those who criticize her beliefs in the supernatural. At a dinner party, she came dressed as a spaceship. After the affair, she was asked how she liked the meal. She jokingly said that it was the best meal she had had in three thousand years.

Many comedians not only laugh at their individual, sometimes painful, personality traits, but they actually emphasize them and make them their trademark.

Woody Allen, for example, jokes about being a loser; he says, "Even in kindergarten, I flunked milk." Phyllis Diller pokes fun at her looks; she says a Peeping Tom once asked her to pull her window shade down. And Rodney Dangerfield wisecracks about his low self-esteem each time he utters his trademark "I don't get no respect."

You might want to consider using some laugh-at-yourself humor to get the upper hand on some of the qualities you may not particularly like about yourself. As the comedians do, you might even want to make it *your* trademark.

I, for example, have been bald since my late high school years. I despaired of my hair falling out at such a young age, but by joking around about it, I have learned to accept it. I now have fun with my "topless" condition by collecting jokes and one-liners that I can use when someone mentions my hairless head. "I'm not bald. I'm just clearing grounds for a new face." "There is one thing to say in favor of baldness: It's neat." I adopted my favorite bit of self-directed humor from comedy writer Robert Orben. I tell people the same thing he does: "I'm a former expert on how to cure baldness."

Any kind of disadvantage or disability becomes less uncomfortable when you can laugh at it before others do. One man who has had a serious stuttering problem for years said it no longer embarrasses him. He can even laugh at the fact that every now and then he will wind up with a double order of lunch—two tuna sandwiches.

John Callahan, a quadriplegic cartoonist, shows others with handicaps that if he can laugh at himself they can laugh at themselves too. In spite of the fact that his cartoons are filled with what many might consider the dark side of life—the disabled, the afflicted, the depressed, and the outcast—Callahan's message is bright. "I want to tell the handicapped to not take it so seriously and to never give up." Paralyzed from the chest down due to a car accident in 1972, Callahan has learned to laugh about the fact that he is in a wheelchair. He says, "I only flirt with girls who look like they have ground-floor apartments."

One of the chapters in the book *Managing Incontinence* suggests that people who suffer with the inability to hold their urine "Try Humor for a Change." At the beginning of the chapter, Cheryle Gartley, the editor, apologizes for including humor in what must be a serious matter for many people. She says not long ago she would have thought that way too. But she has since discovered that "somewhere, hidden in any of the circumstances life hands to us, is a little bit of fun." She asks, "Why not go looking for it?"

Gartley tells the story about Michael, a sixth-grader who went on his first school trip since his artificial sphincter implantation. The class stopped at a fast-food restaurant that was having a big contest promotion. Most of the class knew of

Michael's disability, so they were not surprised when he pointed out that the sign on the wall had a different meaning for them than for him. It read: WIN CONTEST. VOID WHERE PROHIBITED BY LAW.

One man found that laughing at himself first was a good way to deal with his "disability"—he blushes easily. He said you can cover up baldness with a toupee and perhaps medically take care of incontinence, but blushing is difficult, if not impossible, to hide. So when it becomes particularly bad, instead of trying to stop it, which makes it worse, he acknowledges what is happening, pokes fun at himself, and laughs at his inability to control it. He says, "I rate my blushes like a movie critic." I ask those around me, "Do you think this is a number 7 or a number 10 blush?" This sometimes makes him blush even more, but it is easier to handle when framed in the context of a joke.

Abraham Lincoln was a great believer in laugh-at-yourself-and-your-situation humor. When Stephen Douglas accused him of being two-faced, Lincoln said, "If I had two faces, I certainly wouldn't wear this one."

Someone once commented that Lincoln was a very common-looking man. Whereupon he answered, "Friend, the Lord prefers common-looking people. That is the reason he makes so many of them."

Once Lincoln attended a reception in his honor. Upon arriving, he placed his hat on a chair, open side up. Shortly after, a robust lady headed straight for the chair and sat on the hat. Lincoln saw what had happened and rushed over. But it was too late.

Realizing what she had done, the woman got up and handed Lincoln the remains of the hat. "Is this yours?" she asked.

"Yes, it is, ma'am, but I wish you hadn't done that. I could have told you my hat would not fit you before you tried it on."

Being the first to poke fun at your problematic situation is a particularly good technique to use when things go awry. For example, a company representative was giving a group of visitors a tour around the factory. As they approached the testing department, a frustrated employee unable to repair the part he was working on picked it up and hauled it across the room. As the part hit the wall, the embarrassed rep saved the day by proclaiming, "As you can see, all our products are aerodynamically tested before leaving the factory."

In another incident, a salesman was demonstrating his company's machinery just as it malfunctioned. Rather than become all flustered, he recovered quickly and was the first to laugh at the failure. "Well, I guess that concludes my demonstration of my competitor's product for today. I'll be back tomorrow to show you ours."

For years, Gene Perret has been one of Bob Hope's head comedy writers; he is also a three-time Emmy Award winner. But even Perret forgets to laugh at himself once in awhile:

> At one talk I gave, I lost my cool and my sense of humor, and I paid the price.
>
> I flew into Reno to address a luncheon. The sponsors picked me up by limousine and delivered me to the convention hotel in Tahoe, about a ninety-minute ride. I had another date that evening, so it was imperative that I make my flight immediately after my talk.
>
> I checked with the coordinator to make sure there was transportation to the airport. She told me that they couldn't afford another limousine trip, so they made a reservation for me on the shuttle.
>
> I had been on this shuttle before, and it makes several stops. In fact, one time we picked up a woman and her two youngsters from the supermarket, dropped her off at her house, and all the other passengers helped her carry her

groceries inside. I said, "I can't afford to take the chance with the tight travel arrangement I have."

They had no alternative suggestions, so despite my sense-of-humor preaching, I lost my temper. I said, "I'll make my own arrangements without your help, thank you very much."

At the luncheon, I asked if anyone was going to the Reno airport. One doctor graciously offered to expedite his departure and get me to the airport in time for my flight.

I just about made it to the airport with only ten minutes to spare. I rushed to the agent at the gate and said, "Can I make it to the gate in time to get on this flight?" She answered, "You could if you were at the right airport."

I had never checked. They had booked my return flight from the Tahoe airport . . . I would have had plenty of time to make the flight.

I had forgotten my sense of humor and made a fool of myself.

Despite the above, there was a happy ending for Perret. The ticket agent put him on another flight so that he could meet his original connection. She said, "You'll arrive home at the same time and on the correct flight. No one there will ever know what a nincompoop you've been."

Perret says, "I got on my flight chuckling. God bless those with a sense of humor."

It is often difficult for people to laugh at their mistakes, because they are usually embarrassed about them. However, Steve Ettridge, an executive with a Washington, D.C., company, came up with a clever way of helping people get over their embarrassment so that they would fess up. At a management meeting, he put $250 on the table and confessed to a blunder he made. Anyone who could top it could keep the money. Someone did. The procedure has now spread throughout the company and helps people to laugh at themselves and to learn from other people's mistakes. Ettridge himself won the cash for the time he ran out of gas while driving a key job-prospect to the airport.

A visiting-nurses office has also discovered a way to help their employees laugh at themselves and their difficult situations. At each staff meeting they give out a "Tops for the Week" award for the most bizarre story. Patty Wooten said she won one week with her tale about flushing the contents of a bedpan down the john and then watching in horror as the toilet overflowed and gave it all back to her.

Laughing at difficult or embarrassing situations in your life can take the sting out of them. By doing so they cease to have power over you, and others laugh with you instead of at you.

LEARN-TO-LAUGH EXERCISE

Here are two ideas to help you laugh at yourself or your situation:

Look in the mirror. Identify some physical part of yourself that you are not too wild about. Look a little closer and find something in your personality that you are not too crazy about either.

Now see if you can poke a little bit of fun at one of these elements or traits at least once today.

Or, as you go through your day, notice any mistakes you make or mishaps that occur. Can you find some humor in them?

Here are some situations, for example, that might occur in your kitchen and some humorous ways you could laugh about them:

• Dropped an iced cake facedown on the floor? Dust it off and serve it as upside-down cake.

- Didn't notice the butter flying out of the mixer and sticking to the window when you were making cookies? Capitalize on what happened and say you just created "butter-on-the-window cookies."
- Your cake split while cooling? Have a small toy-animal's feet sticking out of the crack and call it an "earthquake cake."

Finding the Advantage
in Your Disadvantage

*Things turn out best for people who make the best of the way
things turn out.*

Art Linkletter

An elderly woman who had been hard of hearing for years
purchased a new hearing aid. When she came back to the
audiologist for a minor adjustment, he said, "Your friends and
relatives must be very pleased that you can hear so well now."
"Oh, I haven't told them," the woman said. "I just sit around
and listen. And you know what? I've changed my will three
times!"

In another instance, a man standing on the street corner
selling "nonbreakable" pens suddenly finds that the one he is
demonstrating with breaks in half. He stops for a moment,
turns to the crowd, and declares, "Now I'll show you what the
inside looks like."

Laughter can turn any disadvantage into an advantage.
People who know this not only look for some positive aspect
in their setbacks but actually go one step further. After their
initial shock, they gather their resources, overcome their problem, and see opportunities where most of us fail to see them.

Moreover, many who have experienced a major loss often
go on to achieve remarkable feats in spite of their ordeal,
because they focus on what they can gain from their circum-
stance rather than on what they have lost. They believe in the

old cliché that every cloud has a silver lining, and they actively seek the advantage in their disadvantage.

Tom Sullivan is one of these people. He has been blind since childhood. In spite of this, he is an athlete, actor, and entertainer. He believes that we all have a handicap of one kind or another—be it shyness, insecurity, old age, or a physical affliction. Tom does not let the handicap of being blind stop him. He has tried his hand at nearly every sport, became proficient at wrestling, and went on to participate in the Olympic Games, the U.S. Nationals, and several world championships.

Once he was wrestling with a fellow from the Soviet Union; the score was 11 to 3, not in Tom's favor. Every time Tom was knocked down, it became more and more painful. Tom had to do something to turn things around. The next time the Russian was on top of him, Tom reached up and popped out one of his own plastic eyes. Seeing the eye lying on the wrestling mat, the Russian immediately let go of Tom and ran out of the ring. In the process, the Russian lost the match, along with everything he had eaten that day.

The record books still note, "Sullivan over Asminov by default."

Seeing some humor in our misfortunes does not make them go away. It does, however, allow us to disengage from our predicament, gather our resources, and not be blinded to our opportunities. Keeping our sense of humor in spite of our disadvantage means that we are able to maintain enough distance between us and our circumstances so that we do not get caught up in our own melodramas.

The most overused words in the news these days are *tragic* and *disaster*. Every time a major event occurs that involves a loss, it is labeled a tragedy. This is not the case with other beings on this planet. When a giraffe approaches a barren tree and finds all the leaves gone, it does not cry out, "My God, what a tragedy! This is a disaster!" Instead, it goes from tree to tree until it locates something to eat.

Many of us have suffered losses that can be called "tragic"—the failure of a business, the amputation of a limb, the destruction of a home. We can hasten the healing of our losses if we see our losses as enriching our life rather than diminishing it. We may not welcome them, but like compost in a garden, our "tragedies" accelerate our growth. "Losing is the price we pay for living," writes Judith Viorst in *Necessary Losses*. "It is also the source of much of our growth and gain."

Often it is the difficult passages in our life that give it meaning and mold us into what we are today. "My experience," says Emmett Miller, a California psychiatrist, "is that those people who have achieved the most in life, who live the richest lives, lives with the most value, lives with the most satisfaction and fulfillment, are people who have faced some catastrophic threat in their lives. The people who are born with the silver spoon in their mouths and never had it taken out are often some of the emptiest, most helpless people I have ever met."

Life is filled with all kinds of losses. We experience them daily. From breaking an arm to having someone break a date with us. From no longer being able to do twenty push-ups to having our vacation trip canceled. From losing our keys to losing a loved one. All loss is significant. All loss can help us grow; there are always lessons to be learned.

In an insightful article published in the *New York Times Magazine*, reporter Richard Shepard writes about losing his wallet. After a period of time, he moves from the first stage of loss, in which he feels like a nonperson without any tangible identity, to a sense of freedom, in which he realizes that he no longer needs to carry around a bundle of infrequently used cards and identity papers.

Shepard did not find much humor in his situation, but he did learn that by losing his wallet, he actually gained something.

According to American Indian tradition, our enemies are sacred because they make us strong. It is our disadvantages—our losses, setbacks, and failures—that can teach us how to become stronger, how to succeed.

Babe Ruth struck out 1,330 times in his baseball career. If he had concentrated on his outs instead of his hits, he would never have been able to set some fifty baseball records, many of which still stand today.

Thomas Edison is another who used failure to succeed. It took him over a thousand tries to discover which filament to use for the incandescent light bulb. "You have failed a thousand times," his critics cried. "Not at all," answered Edison. "What I have done is to discover a thousand materials that don't work."

Failure, according to authors Linda Gottlieb and Carole Hyatt (When Smart People Fail), can help us succeed, because it makes us more courageous to try new things. "In a certain way, failure—real failure—is liberating." Gottlieb, who was fired after being a television and educational film company executive for twenty years, says, "What we all have to do when we fail is to stop dwelling on the one negative thing we did and to retrieve from our past the positive."

It is possible to not only see the lessons in our losses but, as the following story illustrates, also turn a disadvantage around with humor.

Imagine having to give a presentation to a group of clients located about sixty miles from your home. Since you are scheduled to begin your talk very early the next day, you decide it would be easier to avoid the morning rush hour and so drive there the night before. Upon arriving at your destination, you discover that, of the two look-alike suitcases you own, you put the wrong one in the car. The one with your shoes is still at home.

You know you cannot make the presentation in a six-hundred-dollar suit and the beat-up kung fu shoes you have on, so you head for the nearest shopping center. You find that (1) there is no shoe store anywhere in sight and (2) the stores that are there all close in ten minutes.

This scenario actually unfolded before the eyes of business consultant Odette Pollar. She knew she had to find some quick solution and turn her disadvantage into an advantage. So she ran up and down the aisle of the supermarket at the shopping center and grabbed what she thought might get her out of her jam. The next day she told her audience that she had injured herself and gave her seminar with both ankles wrapped in Ace bandages.

In doing research for this book, I noticed that a common phrase kept coming up for people who have gone through painful times. In looking back at their experiences, a number of them said, "It was the best thing that could have happened to me." They did not mean that they had invited the crisis, but that, in hindsight, it had rearranged their priorities, had created a major turning point in their life, and showed them that their disadvantages could be turned around.

Gerald Coffee, a retired navy captain, exemplifies this. He was a prisoner of war for seven years in a cell that allowed him to take only three steps in any direction. Still, his main prayer during these years of unbelievable hardship was, "God, help me use this time to get better." He took a dismal situation and found the advantage in it.

In spite of being able to communicate with his fellow POWs only by tapping on the cell walls, he along with other prisoners managed to learn French, recite Kipling and Shakespeare, and keep their sense of humor. Often he composed poems to keep himself amused. One that he particularly liked went, "Little weevil in my bread, I think I've just bit off your head."

Today Captain Coffee addresses major corporations on the subject of keeping their faith (and sense of humor) during difficult times. He shares his harrowing experience in order to inspire others.

It may seem as if only certain people can turn painful situations into an advantage. Not so. The important thing for all of us to notice in our losses is that every time we lose something, we are presented with an opportunity for a new beginning in each end. Each loss leaves a vacuum, but it also gives us a chance to refill that vacuum. "When one door of happiness closes," said the blind author Helen Keller, "another opens, but often we look so long at the closed door that we do not see the one that has been opened for us."

A Zen poem states this idea in another way: "Since my house burned down," it says, "I now have a better view of the rising moon." Instead of "Oh, shoooot" can come forth an "Ah, so!"

One woman saw this when her house was partially blown away by a tornado. After emerging from the basement, while others thought, "Oh, my God, what a tragedy," she thought, "We were going to move anyway. Now I won't have to pack a thing!"

In *Willard Scott's Down Home Stories*, TV personality Scott tells how humor helped him see an advantage in a disadvantage. He says he used to keep his hairpiece in his desk drawer and put it on just before the broadcast. One time, however, it was gone.

"There was nothing I could do," Scott says, "so I went on the air without it. I announced with a straight face that some dirty dog, some real lowlife, had stolen my hair. We made such a hilariously big deal out of the situation that what could have been a disaster turned into a plus. The following night we enjoyed the best ratings of the season. It seemed everyone in town wanted to see if I would get my hair back."

Author Richard Bach writes in *Illusions* that "there is no such thing as a problem without a gift for you in its hands. You seek problems because you need their gifts." We can begin to see the advantage in the disadvantage when we can focus on the lesson (the gift) instead of the loss.

To close, here is a story about a bird who found his lessons in the most unlikely of places:

> Once upon a time, there was a nonconforming sparrow who decided not to fly south for the winter. Soon the weather turned so cold, however, that he reluctantly started to head south. In a short time ice began to form on his wings and he fell to earth in a barnyard. Just then a cow passed by and crapped on the sparrow. The bird thought it was the end. But the manure warmed him and defrosted his wings. Warm and happy, he started to sing. Just then a cat came by, heard the chirping, cleared away the manure, and ate the bird.

Now, it may seem that there are no lessons here, but there are. In fact, there are three:

1. Everyone who shits on you is not necessarily your enemy.

2. Everyone who gets you out of the shit is not necessarily your friend.

3. If you are warm and happy in a pile of shit, keep your mouth shut.

LEARN-TO-LAUGH EXERCISE

This exercise will help you discover the advantage in the disadvantage.

Are you:

- grieving over your former self while missing the beauty of who you are today?
- depressed because your eyesight is not what it used to be, or are you finding new sight (and perhaps insight) by caressing objects as you never did before?
- angry over the loss of your once luxurious hair, or have you shifted your focus to see that bald is not only beautiful but also means that you never have to waste time fussing and brushing again?

Look back at the upsets and setbacks in your life.
Have any of them opened new doors for you?
Have any made you stronger or wiser?
Have any been a lesson for you?
Have any given you new priorities?

Right now, focus on the positive aspects and the opportunities your upsets, losses, and disadvantages have provided for you.

The World as Your Laff Lab

Life literally abounds in comedy if you just look around you.
Mel Brooks

It takes a serious effort not to be so serious each day, especially when you are experiencing hard times, but it can be done. The biggest deterrent to getting more laughter in your life is you.

You immediately prevent any humor from happening as soon as you say, "I can't because . . ." There would be no *Guinness Book of World Records* if all those people in it had said, "I can't because . . ." Each and every one of them had to overcome some obstacle in order to accomplish what he did.

If you are looking for laughter other than where you are, you will not find it. Your world is your laugh laboratory; you need not look any further.

Someone once asked Willie Sutton, the bank robber, why he robbed banks. Sutton answered, "Because that's where the money is." Look for humor both externally (at work, in your home, in your relationships) and internally (in the things that upset you). There is probably enough humorous material every twenty-four hours in your life for at least a ten-minute stand-up comedy routine.

To find the laughter in your daily dance, pretend that you are a scientist doing humor research. The more things go wrong, the more research material you have for testing your sense of humor. In the interest of science, document how often you can keep your humor when everything is falling apart around you.

An old French proverb says, "The most completely lost of

all days is the one on which we have not laughed." Some days it is harder to laugh than others, but you can get your daily minimum requirement of vitamin H each and every day if you make a conscious effort to do so.

The world is filled with absurdities; find them. In the supermarket, at work, at home, on the bus, on TV, in the newspaper—absurdities abound. I read, for example, about one man who received a bill from a credit card company in the amount of $0.00. He laughed at the bill, showed it to his friends, and then tossed it in the garbage. After several months of continually getting and ignoring the bills, he received one marked "Final Notice"; it threatened credit curtailments and collection agency harassment if he did not pay. So he wrote out a check for no dollars and no cents and sent it off to the company with a note stating, "This pays my account in full."

Shortly after, he received a letter thanking him for his payment and patronage.

Your life, too, is filled with absurdities. Look for them; they are laughable. One of the easiest places to find these is in your mistakes, those bloopers that are an inevitable by-product of being human. Here are some examples:

From student tests:

- "Three kinds of blood vessels are arteries, veins, and caterpillars."
- "To be a good nurse, you must be absolutely sterile."
- "In many states murderers are put to death by electrolysis."

From letters parents wrote to teachers:

- "My son is under doctor's care and should not take fiscal ed. Please execute him."

- "Please excuse Ralph from school on Friday. He had very loose vowels."

From patient medical charts:

- "Discharge status: Alive, but without permission."
- "Skin: Somewhat pale but present."

From a letter received by a county department:

- "I am very much annoyed to find you have branded my son illiterate. This is a dirty lie, as I was married a week before he was born."

At a church service:

- "This being Easter Sunday, we will ask Mrs. Johnson to come forward and lay an egg on the altar."

A final example of a blooper happened when a young nurse misinterpreted a physician's handwriting. He wrote, "Ambulate between bars." She translated the doctor's scribbled message as "Amputate between ears."

As you proceed through the day, open your eyes and ears and collect, be a humor scavenger.

Steve Allen recommends that you read funny books to get some laughs every day. His favorite humorists are Robert Benchley, James Thurber, S. J. Perelman, and Woody Allen. Identify who tickles your funny bone and read what these people have written.

There is also a vast army of anonymous writers who can help you laugh each day. Stop in any greeting-card store and read some of the humorous studio cards. Keep a humor diary and write down funny things that you hear each day. Or look around you for funny signs, bumper stickers, T-shirts, and advertisements. Humor can even be found, as evidenced below, in fortune cookies and on gravestones:

- Bumper sticker: I OWE. I OWE. SO IT'S OFF TO WORK I GO.
- T-shirt slogan: I FINALLY GOT IT ALL TOGETHER AND NOW I FORGOT WHERE I PUT IT.
- Advertisement on the back of a plumber's truck: A FLUSH BEATS A FULL HOUSE.
- Fortune cookie: YOU WILL BE MARRIED WITHIN A YEAR (opened by my seven-year-old daughter).
- Gas station sign: COURTEOUS EFFICIENT SELF-SERVICE.
- Lawn sign: YOUR FEET ARE KILLING ME.
- Gravestone: SEE, I TOLD YOU I WAS SICK.

Some of my biggest laughs have come from printed words that were not actually meant to be funny. One was a coin-laundry sign that read WHEN THE MACHINE STOPS, REMOVE ALL YOUR CLOTHING. Another, at New York's Hayden Planetarium, read TO SOLAR SYSTEM AND REST ROOMS.

What we can learn here is that when our eyes are searching for humor we will find it everywhere. Once when ordering books from a wholesale distributor, I noticed that their catalog listed the following three books in alphabetical order:

Who Am I?
Who Dies?
Who Farted?

I have also found serious-minded signs that were turned into humorous ones. At the top of one of the biggest hills in San Francisco, someone crossed out the words *Steep Hill* and substituted "Cliff." Along a highway that had several signs declaring DEPRESSED STORM DRAINS, someone added "Counseling Will Help." A third appeared (clearly a practical joke) on the door to a ladies room: "PLEASE WAIT TO BE SEATED." While I do not recommend defacing signs, harmless mental graffiti can always turn the mundane into the mirthful.

Another readily available source of humor are the many situation-comedy TV shows, comedy records, videos, and audiotapes. Comedy audiotapes are particularly effective listened to while you are driving in your car. Or find a station that plays comedy on your radio; San Francisco has a daily "Freeway Funnies" show whose airing coincides with the rush hour.

If you like jokes, there are a number of ways of making sure you get your daily chuckle. Use a joke-a-day calendar. Have a joke jar on your desk filled with some of your favorites; take a less-stress break and read one. Tell your friends you are collecting a certain type of joke (light-bulb jokes; clean, wholesome jokes; lawyer jokes; and so on) and watch how many you get.

There is humor all around. "Nothing," says Steve Allen, "is funnier than the unintended humor of reality." Allen writes:

> One way in which I could make a passenger in my car laugh—unless he or she was familiar with the device—was to wait until the first "Your keys are in the ignition," then respond with, "Boy, you can say that again," after which the car would indeed say it again.
>
> The point of this is not to teach you how to make jokes about your "talking car," but rather to encourage an attitude of mind that keeps you on the lookout for the actually or potentially comic factors that are part of daily life.

If you cannot find any humor in your own life, you can learn from people who do and emulate them. On my way to work one day, a woman handed the driver her transfer and proceeded to take a seat in the rear of the bus. The driver looked at the transfer and then called back that the transfer was outdated; it was yesterday's. The young lady turned to the driver and declared, "I know. That's how long I've been waiting for this bus."

You can also get a daily dose of humor in your newspaper. In fact, it can be an interesting challenge to find the funny among the not-so-funny. The same paper that brings you all the "tragic" news in the world also contains the not-so-tragic. Look for it! Read the headlines, but also head for the cartoons and the not-so-serious stuff.

My favorite cartoons are by Gary Larson. Do you recall his cartoon that showed an overhead view of people walking in the park with a bull's-eye target painted on their head? The caption read, "How birds see the world." Discover which are your favorite cartoons and seek them out daily.

There are many ways cartoons can lighten your day:

> **Read them.** Keep a cartoon book by the telephone. Read a couple when you get put on hold.
>
> **Collect them.** File them away and then use appropriate ones in your office memos; it gets your message across, particularly if it is a difficult one, and it makes each memo memorable. (If you are writing about tardiness, for example, consider this Gumpertz cartoon. It says, "Hedgepeth, you went to lunch in 1968. Where have you been?") If you think that your boss might object to cartoons in your memos, remind him that former Secretary of

State George Shultz included a joke in the cables he sent to President Reagan to make sure they got read.

Share them. Start a "Ha-Ha Bulletin Board" at work. Fill it with cartoons and other funny stuff.

Learn from them. You can practice being creative by cutting off the caption of a cartoon and seeing if you can make up your own.

I use this last technique in my workshops to help people sharpen their humor skills; it shows them how they can take an ordinary situation and add some humor to it. One cartoon has a picture of a patient in a hospital gown bending over in a doctor's office and reading a sign on the floor. The original caption read: "You are about to receive your shot." Workshop participants have come up such outrageous captions as, "Crack a smile" and "Congratulations, you're mooning the entire waiting room."

Cartoons are not the only humor to be found in the newspaper. Often the news itself is so bizarre that it is laughable. What we can learn when we read these stories is that we live in a crazy, laughable world, so maybe we need to take it and ourselves less seriously. Here, for example, are just a few items that appeared in the newspapers within a short period of time:

- A California judge ruled that a man on trial for being an accessory to murder could go free because he was actually the murderer and thus could not be his own accessory.
- A city in Michigan spent $50,000 on new flagpoles and then ran out of money, so could not afford flags for them.

- A "Buy Britain" essay contest in England gave out radios made in Japan as prizes.

- The International Banana Association complained that an AIDS documentary that used a banana to demonstrate the proper use of a condom would blemish the banana's image.

The *New York Times* ran a "can-you-believe-this-one?" story about a man who was trying to do a good deed by clipping a dead limb from the tree in front of his apartment building. He cut his hand, fell out of the tree, and landed on top of a passerby. The pedestrian thought he was being attacked so he slugged the pruner, who staggered into the street, where he just missed being hit by a taxi. Dazed, the pruner just started to get his footing when he was brought down by a neighborhood dog that bit him and tore his pants.

The newspaper even has humor in the classifieds. This ad was found in the *Belle Fourche Daily Post*: "Lost—Dog, faded brown, three legs, one ear missing, blind left eye, broken tail, recently neutered. Answers to name 'Lucky.' Sorry, no rewards."

One classified ad actually turned into an unusual news story. A woman jokingly ran an ad to sell her husband. It read:

Husband for Sale, Cheap—Comes complete with hunting and fishing equipment, one pair of jeans, two shirts, boots, black Labrador retriever and fifty pounds of venison. Pretty good guy, but not home much from October to December and April to October. Will consider a trade.

The large volume of calls she received prompted her to run a retraction. The following day's paper read:

Retraction of "Husband for Sale, Cheap." Everybody wants the dog, not the husband.

There is, indeed, humor all around us. For example, a young violinist came out of the subway in New York City, approached a policeman, and asked, "Could you please tell me how to get to Carnegie Hall? The officer looked in the eyes of the young man with the violin case and answered, "Practice, my son, practice!"

The three key words for finding and getting more laughter in your life are: *practice*, *practice*, *practice*.

One humorist told me that he would not perform a joke on stage unless he had told it forty times offstage. It took Lily Tomlin five years to perfect her Broadway show *The Search for Signs of Intelligent Life in the Universe*. Comedians know how to *be* funny because they practice; but if you want to *see* funny, you need to practice too. It's like learning a foreign language; to be a proficient humor finder, you need to persist.

One final word. In doing your humor research, remember to be gentle with yourself. Start slow. Try a smile first. Then maybe a chuckle. They are all preparation for tomorrow's full-blown belly laugh. And remember, give yourself rewards, pats on the back, and standing ovations just for trying.

LEARN-TO-LAUGH EXERCISE

This final exercise asks that you make a commitment to get more laughter in your life and your losses.

There is a proverb that goes, "I know all about swimming, but doing it is another matter." Unless you begin to incorporate some of the techniques suggested here for getting more humor, laughter, and play in your life, the knowledge you have will not do you any good.

Are you ready to make a humor commitment?

Are you willing to put it down on paper?

If you are, then write yourself the following letter:

Dear _____ ,

    The one thing I am going to do to get more laughter in my life is _____ .

Sincerely,

_____

P.S. If I have accomplished the above, I will reward myself with _____ .

Adding more laughter to your life takes work and determination. Reward yourself for doing such a great job. Celebrate your success by giving yourself some small reward—like a Cadillac, or maybe a Mercedes.

PART

III

The Last Laugh

Sometimes we do not see the importance of laughter in our dark times because we are so blinded by our tears.

I am convinced, however, that if we only had an instant replay of our actions from time to time, we would be able to laugh with ourselves more than we do. If we could only step back and see how purposeless our seriousness is in so many instances, we might also learn to laugh more. If we could only step back and see our problems in relation to life's larger picture it would, as humor does, help put them in perspective.

An anonymous author once wrote:

My life is but a weaving between my Lord and me,
I cannot chose the colors, He weaveth steadily.
Sometimes He weaveth sorrow, and I in foolish
   pride,
Forget He sees the upper and I the underside.
Not 'til the loom is silent and the shuttle cease
   to fly,
Shall God unroll the canvas and explain the reason
   why.

The dark threads are as needful in the weaver's
  skillful hands,
As the ones of gold and silver in the path that He
  has planned.

When I look back at my wife's death, I realize that one of the greatest lessons she left me, and one that I now share with you, is "Life is too short to concentrate on the dark threads; look for, celebrate, and enjoy the ones of gold and silver."

In addition to laughing at life's ongoing daily hassles, we can also learn to take the processes at the end of life—illness, death, and grief—less seriously. Laughing in the face of death provides the same much-needed physical and psychological benefits that laughter gives us at other, less oppressing times. Humor during such trying moments as death, grieving, and illness is of benefit to both the person going through the loss as well as for those around them—the family, friends, and professional care-givers.

Remaining open to levity even in the most solemn situations can help survivors stay both mentally and physically healthy. Being overly serious in the grieving process can be deadly. One study, for example, showed that the immune systems of grieving spouses had lower activity levels of T cells—one of the body's defenses against illness. Another study in Finland reported that the overall death rate among the bereaved during the first year of loss was more than double the normal rate.

Humor and laughter can physically help keep our immune system in balance and psychologically help us cope and communicate at a time when coping is, at best, difficult and communication often at a standstill.

One Chinese proverb states, "You cannot prevent the birds of sorrow from flying over your head, but you can prevent them from building nests in your hair." The techniques suggested earlier not only lighten up our everyday trials and losses but can also lighten up our larger ones and prevent those nests from forming.

"You can grieve for a loss," says Dr. Bernie Siegel, "yet still keep yourself from losing all perspective, all appreciation for the good things that remain in your life." Humor serves this purpose. It gives perspective and keeps us in balance when life seems out of balance.

No matter how serious the situation, it is possible to keep our perspective. As observed by Rabbi Harold Kushner in his best-seller, *When Bad Things Happen to Good People*, "We need to get over the questions that focus on the past and on the pain—'Why did this happen to me?'—and ask instead the question that opens doors to the future: 'Now that this has happened, what shall I do about it?' "

While working with the seriously ill and the grieving, I saw that humor helped people do something about their physical and mental discomforts. It helped them look at a negative period in their lives in a more positive way. Humor gave them a choice. It showed them that they did not have to be so stuck in their predicaments. It showed them that they did not have to be blinded by pain and suffering.

I sometimes saw laughter squelched, however, because people thought that anything connected to death and dying had to be "serious." It need not be. In fact, any nurse or undertaker will tell you that humorous incidents frequently occur around intense death-related situations. What is important for all of us to remember is not to close ourselves off and exclude laughter because we think death *must* be solemn.

One of the biggest difficulties people have in adding levity to their grave situations is the lack of permission they give themselves or get from others. It is important to look for humor in the dying and grieving process and to give ourselves and others permission to laugh in the face of death.

"Weeping and feeling depressed at times is natural, but it drains you," says Vera Kiley, whose daughter was shot and paralyzed. In *Beyond Survival*, by Theresa Saldana, Kiley notes, "On the other hand, laughing and being happy makes you feel energized. So we—the families and friends—appreciate it so much when people allow us to let down our hair, to smile and relax awhile and to enjoy ourselves in spite of it all."

Encouraging you to look for humor in what appears to be a humorless situation by no means implies that humor need be the main focus during these times. Expressions of less joyous emotions are also important. Nor is laughter always appropriate. I only mean this: First, loss is part of life; it is neither sad nor funny. And second, we often forget how beneficial laughter can be during our dark times.

Various cultures and religious traditions acknowledge that there is no need to remain solemn around loss. In fact, there is good reason not to. They teach that when we can see some humor in difficult times, even in our death-related losses, it takes away some of the sting of those events.

For example, several tribes in West Africa assign someone to restrain, entertain, and distract the bereaved. In his study of these mortuary customs, anthropologist Jack Goody notes that in the three days that precede the burial of the dead, this "joking partner" helps shift the emphasis from "restraining the grief of the bereaved to promoting the opposite reaction, laughter."

The Jewish tradition too encourages the benefits of laughter in painful times. Life is hard, but it also is to be enjoyed; times may be bad, but that does not mean we must have a bad time. If we are to see good times, we are told, we must survive the bad.

"If we could hang all our sorrows on pegs and were allowed to choose those we like best, every one of us would take back his own, for all the rest would seem even more difficult to bear." This Hasidic saying illustrates how the Jews teach that our life may not be all that we want, but it is all that we have. Therefore when asked, "Does your heart ache?" the Jew immediately knows the answer. He responds, "Laugh it off."

CHAPTER 3

Less of a Grave Matter

The town of Chelm was known as the town of fools. One day, someone asked one of the elders which was more important, the sun or the moon.

The elders pondered the question for a long time and then replied, "The moon. The moon is more important. After all," they said, "the moon shines at night when we really need the light, while the sun shines during the day when there is already plenty of light."

We become so overwhelmed by illness, death, and grief that we forget that humor, like the moon, can bring relief to our darkest times.

Unfortunately, when ill or in the dying process, people forget this. They constantly focus on the pain and suffering. When we are ill, for example, everyone wants to know, "How are you doing?" The concern may be gratifying, but nothing could be more discouraging or draining than to have to constantly repeat our prognosis over and over again.

Dana Gribben, a communication expert, humorously solved the problem of repeating why her leg was in a cast and how she was doing. "I knew," she says, "that many people would be curious about my knee, which I injured while doing back flips off some playground equipment, so I made up a sign and put it into the plastic name-tag holder I had from some convention. It read: THANK YOU FOR ASKING. MY KNEE IS DOING BETTER. I FEEL OKAY, AND YES, IT DOES HURT. The note ended: THE PROGNOSIS IS UNKNOWN. CHECK HERE FOR UPDATES IN THE FUTURE.

Another man, who lost a toe in a lawn-mower accident, humorously solved the problem of informing people what happened by making up a different story each time. He told one child that he was stranded on a desert island and got so hungry that he ate it. His favorite line was that it fell off when he got "toe-main" poisoning.

Norman Cousins believes that part of the responsibility of creating humor lies with the patient. After all, when we are hurting, if we can make others laugh and feel better, then we often feel better too. When Cousins was in the hospital, he says, "The nurse came in with a specimen bottle at a time when I was having breakfast. While she wasn't looking, I took my apple juice, poured it in the bottle, and handed it to her. She looked at it and said, 'We're a little cloudy today, aren't we?' " Taking a swig from the bottle, Cousins answered, "By George, you're right; let's run it through again."

Writer Wilson Mizner also added humor to his hospital stay. When the nurse wrote his name, illness, and other information on his chest for identification purposes before he was about to go into surgery, he took the marker and added a postscript: "Store in a cool place until opened."

In serious illness, we forget how uplifting humor can be for the patient and how important it is in helping him deal with both the physical and psychological losses being undergone.

In the dying process, humor provides two additional benefits. It helps us cope with the anxieties we have about our own demise, and it helps those involved with the dying—the families, friends, and professional care-givers—come to terms with their loss.

LOOKING FOR LAUGHTER IN LOSS

I think we're finally at a point where we've learned to see death with a sense of humor.

Katharine Hepburn

In order for family, friends, health-care workers, and the patient to see some humor in their trying times, they need to look for the absurdities that frequently occur during intense death-related situations.

One place to find these absurdities is in the unexpected. Art Gliner, a humorist from Silver Spring, Maryland, relates being called to the hospital after his father died. "For some reason," he said, "the nurse handed me a plastic container that held my father's teeth. I had carried that container around with me for fifteen or twenty minutes to different parts of the hospital before I realized what I was holding. As I saw the absurdity in this, I turned to my brother-in-law and remarked, 'I never go anywhere without my father's teeth.'"

I learned to look for the humor in the unexpected when I was a volunteer with the Hospice of San Francisco. Once I visited a woman who was always dozing on the couch while her TV blared. Our total conversation in the three times I saw her consisted of "Hello" when I arrived and "Good-bye" when I left. On my fourth visit, I was determined to do something. I said, "Mrs. Krantz, I am here to help you. Isn't there something I can do?" She looked at me and asked, "Do you know how to dance?"

Being a "helper," I wanted to do whatever I could for her, so I got up and danced around the room to the music of *The Dating Game*, which was playing on the tube. Thinking I had made a bit of headway, I inquired if there was anything else I could do. She asked me to disco. Again, wanting to please her, I obliged, and disco danced around the room. When I finished, I asked if she had enjoyed it. She shrugged her shoulders. Feeling frustrated, I inquired once again, "Are you sure there is nothing else I can do? I'm here to help you."

She thought for a moment and then replied, "Yes, there is something you can do. You can leave!"

Devastated, I returned to the hospice office and told my sad story. Immediately, my co-workers started to roar with laughter. "Imagine a camera in the corner of that room, filming you disco dancing to *The Dating Game!*" When I got the picture, I starting guffawing too.

Another example concerns a hospice patient who was having a particularly bad day. When she said, "I think I am dying," a small picture of Jesus and a single candle were brought into the room. The attendant and the family began to pray. After a while they looked up to discover the picture, which had caught fire from the candle, in flames. Everyone in the room burst out laughing—including the patient, who later rallied for a period.

Frequently, humor will arise out of an unexpected juxtaposition of wry comment and serious situation. Comedian Michael Pritchard tells a true story about a man who, throughout his life, continually told other people how to do things. One morning he died in his upstairs bedroom. When the undertakers came to remove the corpse, they had great difficulty maneuvering the massive, overweight body around the bend at the top of the stairs. At one point it actually got stuck between the wall and the banister. Just then, one of the distressed family members looked up from below and uttered, "Come on, Dad, tell us what to do now!"

One patient I was working with said, "I don't want to die, but when I do, I want my ashes put in some paint and the bedroom repainted with it." When I inquired why, she replied, "Then I can look down from the ceiling and see if there is any hanky-panky going on here."

In his introduction to Dan Keller's book *Humor as Therapy*, psychotherapist Gerald Piaget writes about how a juxtaposition of a humorous comment and his client's contemplation of suicide actually helped her have second thoughts about taking her own life. His patient, Carol, told him:

> Well, I was feeling horrible. You were gone, my husband was in no mood to hear more bitching, and I was really depressed. So I called Joan [Piaget's wife and Carol's best friend] to talk. During our conversation, I mentioned that with the cancer, and the depression, and the uncertainty and all, maybe there was no use even going on.
>
> I said it sort of casually, but in truth thoughts of suicide had been coming up for a couple of days. Now, Joan knows I'm not the suicidal type, but she got really angry at me.
>
> "Damn it, Carol!" she yelled. "If you dare kill yourself I swear to Christ I'll go to that cemetery and piss all over your grave!"
>
> That image hasn't worn off, at least not yet. You know this hasn't been a very good week for me. But whenever I think of killing myself, I get this ridiculous image of Joan out there in the graveyard, with her eyes angry and her lower lip stuck out and her skirt hiked up around her waist, just squatting there on my grave. . . . It lightens me up, and I just don't feel like dying anymore. . . .

Another place to look for humor in a death-related situation is in the ambiguities that surround the dying process. The avalanche of mixed emotions here can create fertile ground for comic moments.

In an edition of *Ladies' Home Journal*, for example, Carol Willis, a woman dying of cancer, wrote:

> I'm still angry about it all, for I think no one has ever loved living more or had more fun doing it than I, and I want it to go on and on. But if I can't, then I must be truthful and

say there are a few advantages in living only half a lifetime. Besides the end of good, death also means the end of tribulations—no more holding in the stomach, no more P.T.A., no more putting up the hair in pin curls, no more Cub Scouts, no more growing old.

In another case, where the ambiguities of dying produced some humor, a hospice patient who was very near death refused to eat any more food; she said that she wanted to die. The following day, she announced her intention to die again, and again the day passed without her demise. This went on for several days. Then one day she arose from her bed and joined the rest of the family at the breakfast table. The amazed family members wanted to know why she was joining them for breakfast after so many days of fasting. The frail, elderly lady turned and answered, "I've changed my mind about eating. After all, who wants to die on an empty stomach?"

Sometimes simply doing or saying something nonsensical can lighten up the heaviest of circumstances. Maria, for example, a teacher of Hispanic origin, tells of her father who lay dying in a hospital. He was given four to six weeks to live by the physicians. As was the custom in their family, members came dressed in black and sat silently among the dozens of floral arrangements with burning candles all around. Maria said, "When I came to visit him, he looked up at me, quite alert, and motioned for me to come to his bedside. I gazed around the room at all the flowers and silent figures and took his hand and whispered, 'Dad, who died?' He smiled at me and said, 'I wish I knew.' "

Dr. Simonton recalls how he used a bit of nonsense to lighten things up after the death of his father. Because his father was a prominent man in the community, Simonton was overwhelmed by condolence callers. Just as he started to feel uplifted, another grieving person would bring him down again. To turn things around, he placed a rubber cookie on the plate of real ones. When a guest tried to eat the fake one, the somber atmosphere suddenly was broken. The rubber cookie, says Simonton, has become a permanent symbol of his father's death.

I, too, have successfully employed some absurd nonsense to lighten up a situation. When my dog became ill, I took her to the veterinarian, who treated and discharged her. Within two days, she became noticeably worse, so I called the vet again and was told to rush her in for emergency surgery. Since she was old and so seriously ill, I anticipated that this might be the last time I would see her alive; as it turned out, I was right. The ride to the hospital was difficult, but I deliberately tried to ease the tension with humor. While my friend Dave was driving, I held Rifka's paw and taught her visualizations. "Okay, Rifka, visualize your tummy healing. See your tumor getting smaller. See yourself chasing squirrels in the park. See yourself eating a banana." I knew that the suggestions probably did not help the dog, but the moment of laughter sure helped Dave and me.

Another place death-related humor can be found is in our efforts to circumvent straightforward mention of dying or burial. In an effort to do so, we have unknowingly created a large number of euphemisms, many of them humorous.

I am not sure if these help us face death or even lighten it up, but it is amusing to consider the absurd lengths we have gone to in order to avoid even mentioning *the word*. The source from which I selected the words below (*American Speech,*) lists nearly 400 items that can replace the words *death* or *dying.*

Some sound like an AT&T commercial:
called home
called beyond
heard the final call
his number was up

Some sound like you are leaving a hotel:
    cashed his checks
    checked out
    exited
Some are so misleading they don't really indicate
what is happening:
    striked out
    shuffled off
    kicked the bucket
    stepped off the deep end
    bit the dust
    is pushing up the daisies
One intrinsically sounds funny:
    croaked
Another sounds physically impossible to accomplish:
    met his end
And one even sounds slightly off-color:
    petered out

One clergyman, the article relates, overdid his euphemisms. During a funeral service, he pointed to the corpse and said, "This is only the shell—the nut is gone."

The absurdities of life and death constantly surround us. During times of loss, as at other times, we can look for them or ignore them. The choice is ours.

HUMOR, ILLNESS, AND DEATH: YOU'VE GOT TO BE KIDDING

Life does not cease to be funny when people die any more than it ceases to be serious when people laugh.
                                                    George Bernard Shaw

HELPING THE HELPER

For the family and friends of the terminally ill or deceased, humor can be a source of strength and courage. Laughter in the grieving process is a sign of emergence from grief and depression. It is an indication that the survivor is beginning to embrace life again, that healing is taking place.

"No matter how great your pain," says Earl Grollman in *What Helped Me When My Loved One Died*, "there is hope and help for the future. As your sense of humor returns and you find yourself laughing, you're feeling better."

Laura, a young woman in her late twenties, is a good example of someone who knows the value of humor in times of loss. Her brother died when she was very young, her father died of a terminal illness a number of years before I met her, and her mother had recently been killed in a car crash. Although she had three people close to her die, Laura felt that humor acted as a booster to cut through the heaviness of her losses.

When her father was dying, Laura said that "it wasn't very pleasant sitting at the dinner table, trying to have a decent meal, and have my father pass some gas. He would lean forward in his chair and say, 'Pardon me, one cheek-sneak coming out of the left.' We hated the fact that the room was going to smell, but we loved that he could joke about it."

Laura said that her father had been a very funny man throughout his life. Even when near death, he insisted on attending a Halloween party. With his loss of hair, loss of weight, and yellowed skin, he had the perfect physique for the disguise he had in mind. He wrapped a sheet around himself, fashioned a pair of glasses out of a coat hanger, and attended the party as Mahatma Gandhi.

For Laura, it was important that her father's joking spirit did not stop when he became ill or even after he was gone. So when her family was selecting a coffin, she got everyone giggling when she suggested that they have a slumber party in the casket room.

Along with the many upsetting and depressing moments in the dying process can also be some lighter ones. "I was surprised how much joy I could find in that little house with my friend dying in the living room," says author Deborah Duda in her book *A Guide to Dying at Home.* While working with Mary, a fifty-year-old woman with cancer, Duda says, "There was joy in our jokes about our spiritual interests or my using her as an excuse to get out of meetings I didn't want to go to—and in our "waltzing." When Mary couldn't walk alone anymore, I held her up under the arms. I'd ask, "Madam, may I have this waltz?" Our silliness let her know she wasn't a burden and helped her release some of the frustration of no longer being able to walk alone."

For professional care-givers, who encounter numerous deaths, humor can be a way of releasing their own feelings of frustration and helplessness. Unfortunately, families and patients often feel this attitude is less than professional—"How can you laugh at a time like this?" What they do not realize is the importance humor can have for the care-giver. In an article abridged from the *American Journal of Nursing*, Wayne Johnston, the chief anesthetist at Douglas Jarman Hospital in Tuscola, Illinois, addresses this:

You saw me laugh after your father died.

I was splashing water on my face at a sink midway between the emergency room lobby where you stood and the far green room where his body lay. Someone told a feeble joke and I brayed laughter like a jackass, decorum forgotten until I met your glance over the physician's gray flannel shoulder—your eyes streaming tears. . . .

My laugh was inappropriate, and for that I apologize. But it was, nonetheless, a necessity. . . .

All of us worked damn hard. We intubated, oxygenated, monitored, massaged, shocked, injected. And in our own ways, we prayed. Nothing helped. After forty minutes the physician said to stop. We stood uneasily, avoiding each other's eyes. We began to remove our puny and now futile tubes and wires, slowly, in awe of death, as always. And in silent sorrow. . . .

Being human . . . we all sooner or later laugh at the wrong time. I hope your father would understand that my laugh meant no disrespect. . . .

That day you saw me laugh, I knew that another patient was waiting who needed my care and full attention in surgery. As I stood at that sink and washed sweat and vomitus from my face and arms, my laugh was no less cleansing for me than your tears were for you.

HELPING THE PATIENT

For the patient, humor can be a way of coping with failing body functions, unfamiliar medical procedures, and confused emotions.

It can help the patient step back from the illness, offer a brief reprise, and aid in showing that there is more to life than just physical disability. Humor validates the fact that although someone may be seriously ill or in the process of dying, for the moment at least, he or she is still alive.

When someone is seriously ill, we frequently allow illness to crowd out everything else. We tend to forget they are more than just their disease. Unknowingly, we separate ourselves. But a few chuckles shared between the two parties changes that. "Laughter," said comedian Victor Borge, "is the shortest distance between two people." Shared laughter between a patient and someone else is like saying, "If we can laugh together, then I am no different than you. Even though you may be ill, or dying, we still have something in common."

When people are going through trying times, we can support them by encouraging their humor and help them see things in a lighthearted way.

People magazine, for example, reported on a powerful and playful way of supporting someone who was experiencing a major life crisis. When Manuel Garcia lost his hair after undergoing chemotherapy for stomach cancer, his brother and three relatives shaved their heads in support of Garcia's hairless pate. After Manuel arrived home, nearly fifty friends and relatives shaved their heads too. A few weeks later, the total had risen to one hundred clean-shaven heads.

We cannot all go around shaving our heads, but there are mirthful ways of supporting others, or asking others to support us, when life is hanging in the balance:

Going to visit someone in the hospital? Bring a "joy bag" filled with small toys, games, funny books, photos, and special mementos. (Going to be a hospital patient yourself? Remember to pack some things that amuse you or make you smile.)

Decorate a sterile hospital room with funny signs, sayings, or posters.

Decorate *yourself.* If you think the patient is up to it, walk into the room wearing Groucho glasses or a clown nose.

Supply the patient with a small cassette player, earphones, and a batch of comedy tapes.

If stitches make laughter uncomfortable, ask the patient to try smiling several times an hour.

If possible, have the patient keep a diary of all the funny and absurd things that occur in conjunction with the illness. (Did someone wake him or her up to administer a sleeping pill?)

Remember that a patient is more than his or her illness. Do not continually focus on the illness.
After you get a progress report, steer conversations to the lighter side.

Finally, remember, too, that although laughter is contagious, there are such things as off-days, and this just may not be the right one for mirth. Try again another time.

The idea of keeping a hospital diary is a particularly good one, since it can help the patient focus on the absurdly funny incidents that inevitably occur in hospital settings. Alison Crane, executive director of the American Association for Therapeutic Humor, recounts one story originally told to her by a middle-aged pastor.

I had a very serious accident a few years ago; it was amazing I survived. And, of course, I was in the hospital for a very long time recuperating.

Because I was there for so long, I became rather non-chalant with the nurses about the procedures they subjected me to—you can't keep decorum up for very long with no clothes on. I was also having trouble finding a relatively painless spot to put yet another injection of pain medication. . . .

One time I rang for the nurse, and when she came on the intercom, I told her I needed another pain shot. I knew it would take just about as long for her to draw up the medication as it would for me to gather the strength to roll over and find a spot for her to inject it. I had succeeded in rolling over, facing away from the door, when I heard her come in. "I think this area here isn't too bad," I said, pointing to an exposed area of my rear. But there was an awful silence after I said that. My face paled as I rolled over slowly to see who had actually come in—it was one of my twenty-two-year old female parishioners! I apologized and tried to chat with her, but she left shortly thereafter, horribly embarrassed.

Well, about thirty seconds after she left, the impact of the situation hit me and I started to laugh. It hurt like you can't imagine, but I laughed and laughed and laughed. Tears were rolling down my face and I was gasping when my nurse finally came in. She asked what had happened. I tried to tell her, but couldn't say more than a word or two before convulsing into laughing fits again. Amused, she told me she would give me a few minutes to calm down and she'd be back to give me my shot.

I had just started to regain my composure when my nurse reappeared and asked again what had happened. I started to tell her, got to laughing again, and she started to laugh just from watching me, which made it worse. Finally, she left again, promising to try back in fifteen more minutes. This scenario repeated itself a couple of more times, and by the time I could tell her what had happened, I felt absolutely no pain. None. I didn't need medication for three more hours. And I know it was an emotional turning point in my recovery.

CHAPTER 4

To Die Laughing

*The one serious conviction that a man should have is that
nothing is to be taken too seriously.*

—Samuel Butler

LESSONS FROM RELIGIOUS
TRADITIONS AND OTHER CULTURES

Our culture has taught us to view death as our enemy. We can,
however, see the dying process differently and learn to lighten
up about it by looking at the teachings of religious traditions
and cultures that do not view death as ominously as we do, at
laugh-makers who do not treat death as a taboo subject, and
at those people who have come in contact with either their
own death or that of others and have still been able to maintain
their sense of humor.

*When one has understanding one should laugh; one should
not weep.*

Zen saying

In death, as in life, our attitudes are the crayons that color the
world.

We can see illness as a hopeless time or as a chance to slow
down and take stock of our life. We can see death as an unfair
end to life or as a necessary part of it. We can see grief as

182

inescapable or as an opportunity for us to gather our resources and move on. We can see funerals as a time to lash out at death or to celebrate life.

Both Zen and Jewish traditions see pain, suffering, and death as part of life and therefore embrace them with a laugh that at once reduces the pain and teaches us not to take anything in life too seriously. Both are saying the same thing: Every situation, every experience—even death—is ripe for humor. Here is an example from the Jewish tradition:

"Ladies and gentlemen," the manager announces. I am terribly sorry to have to tell you that the great actor Yankel Leib has just had a stroke, and we cannot go on with tonight's performance."

At this, a woman in the second balcony stands and cries, "Quick, give him an enema!"

"Lady," says the manager, "the stroke was fatal."

"So give him an enema!" she shouts once more.

"Lady, you don't understand. Yankel Leib is dead; an enema can't possibly help."

"It certainly couldn't hurt!"

Humor cannot stop us from dying, but as the lady in the second balcony (as well as the Zen and Jewish traditions) remind us, "it certainly couldn't hurt." Humor may not alter the fact that we die; but it helps us live with it and deal with it.

Both Zen and Jewish traditions teach us that laughter offers us new perspectives on our fears. Any loss, therefore, even complete annihilation, as in the story below, can be turned around with a laugh:

A new flood is foretold and nothing can be done to prevent it; in three days, the waters will wipe out the world.

The leader of Buddhism appears on television and pleads with everybody to become a Buddhist; that way, they will at least find salvation in heaven.

The Pope goes on television with a similar message. "It is still not too late to accept Jesus," he says.

The chief rabbi of Israel takes a slightly different approach: "We have three days to learn how to live under water."

Zen teaches how to lighten up our dark times with a quiet approach; it uses thought-provoking stories and koans—those nonsensical questions that have many answers and at the same time none. ("What is the sound of one hand clapping?") Judaism, on the other hand, is somewhat more down-to-earth. ("Cancer-schmancer! As long as you're healthy.")

Jews joke about the inevitability of death by reminding us that "for dying you always have time." The Zen teachings do likewise and lightheartedly remind us of an important lesson. Everything, they tell us in the story below, dies.

Ikkyu, the Zen master, was very clever even as a boy. His teacher had a precious teacup, a rare antique. Ikkyu happened to break this cup and was greatly perplexed. Hearing the footsteps of his teacher, he held the pieces of the cup behind him. When the master appeared, Ikkyu asked: "Why do people have to die?"

"This is natural," explained the older man. "Everything has to die and has just so long to live."

Ikkyu, producing the shattered cup, added, "It was time for your cup to die."

Zen and Judaism are not the only traditions to teach death-and-dying lessons through humorous tales. The devilishly clever character named Mulla Nasrudin, for example, is often used by the Sufis for this same purpose. Here is one Nasrudin tale that again reminds us of the universal fact that everything dies.

One day Nasrudin went to his neighbor and asked to borrow a very large pot. "I am sorry," said the neighbor, "I cannot lend you my pot. I fear that it will not be returned."

Nasrudin assured the neighbor that in exactly three days he would bring it back. The neighbor finally agreed.

Three days later, to the minute, Nasrudin appeared with the pot. When the neighbor looked inside, to his surprise, there was another tiny pot.

"What is this?" asked the neighbor.

"While your pot was at my house," replied Nasrudin, "it gave birth."

A week later Nasrudin appeared again at his neighbor's house wanting to borrow the large pot. This time the neighbor was more than pleased to lend it to him, providing Nasrudin would again bring it back in three days. Nasrudin agreed.

Three days passed and there was no sign of either Nasrudin or the pot. When he and his neighbor met at the market later that week, the neighbor inquired about his pot.

"I am sorry to tell you, but your pot died."

"My pot died?" asked the neighbor. How can that be? Pots do not die."

"If pots give birth," replied Nasrudin, "pots die."

From China comes another story to help us deal with our death fears. As told in the fairy tale below, not only must everything die, but it does so for a reason. Death as part of a larger picture is a necessary part of life. Without it, life would not only be totally different than it is now, but most probably also totally unmanageable.

Once upon a time, a great king went hunting with his closest companions. They paused at the top of a hill from which they could see for miles around. As the king surveyed his domain, with its rich fields and bustling cities, tears came to his eyes. He thought of his palaces and friends, the honor and wealth that belonged to him, and the love of his people. "To think that one day I must die, and leave all this behind!" the king lamented. The nobles with him started thinking, and soon they began commiserating with their king: they, too, would lose palaces, riches, and honors when they died.

"Imagine if we could live forever!" the king said. "Aye," his nobles agreed, their eyes bright at the thought of immortality. One lord among them laughed. "We should never have to leave all this," the king went on, ignoring the interruption, but the noble laughed again. This happened several more times, until the king himself demanded the reason for the mirth. Then the lord bowed. "I cannot keep my joke from you, Majesty," he confessed, "although I hesitate to say it." The lord paused and went on.

"I imagined what it would be like if we all lived forever, and if there were no death," the lord explained. "Why then, the First King would still live among us, and the Great Sage! The Immortal Emperor, and the Fearless General, too! Compared with them, I and my fellow lords would be fit only to be rice-planters, and you, Majesty, would be a clerk! Imagining that, I could not help laughing!"

The other lords held their breaths, fearing the king's wrath. After a tense moment, the king laughed. He raised his drinking glass and turned to the other lords. "For encouraging my foolishness, I penalize each of you a drink of wine! And as for you," the king told the laughing lord, "whenever I bewail my death again, you are to cry out, 'A clerk! A clerk!' "

We may not want death at the end of life, but there is not much we can do about it except enjoy what we have while we have it. Even in our darkest moments, even when death is imminent, even if we are hanging on to life by a thread, we still, as this final Zen story teaches, can look around and find something to enjoy!

A man traveling across a field suddenly encounters a tiger. The man flees as the tiger runs after him. Coming to a precipice, the man takes hold of the root of a large, wild vine and swings himself over the edge. The tiger sniffs at him from above. Trembling, the man looks down and discovers that another tiger below is waiting to eat him should he fall. The only thing that holds the man up is the vine, and it is now being gnawed at by two mice near the top of the cliff.

As the man looks around at his predicament, he sees a luscious strawberry on a nearby branch. Grasping the vine with one hand, he plucks the strawberry with the other.

"How sweet it tastes!" he says.

LESSONS FROM LAUGH-MAKERS

Death is always with us; creative art helps us know it, live with it, and even laugh at it.

Dr. Robert Litman,
"Grave Humor," *A Celebration of Laughter*

Comedy writers, comics, and cartoonists help us see demise through humorous eyes. They get us to laugh at something we generally think is not a laughing matter. In doing so, they help relieve some of our death-related anxieties, as illustrated in the following classic joke:

Mr. Pinsky persuaded his brother to take care of his Siamese cat while he was on an overseas business trip. Mr. Pinsky dearly loved this cat, but the brother did not. The very moment Pinsky returned from his trip, he called his brother to find out about the cat. The brother announced abruptly, "Your cat is dead," and hung up.

For days Pinsky was inconsolable. Finally, he was able to telephone his brother again. "It was needlessly cruel and uncaring of you to tell me so abruptly that my cat had passed away."

"What did you expect me to do?" blared the brother.

"You could have broken the news more gently," said Pinsky. "First, you could have said that the cat was playing on the roof. Later you could have told me he fell off. The next morning you could have called back and said that he broke his leg. Then, when I came to pick him up, you could have told me that he passed away during the night. But I guess you don't have it in you to be so civilized. Now, tell me, how's Mama?"

The brother waited a moment, then announced, "She's playing on the roof."

According to author George Mikes, laughing at death gives us triple pleasure: "The pleasure of the joke itself, the malicious joy of laughing at death's expense, and the pleasure of taming Death and fraternizing with him."

Many of Gary Larson's "The Far Side" cartoons create this triple pleasure. One shows a man in an electric chair waiting to be electrocuted while his executioners fiddle with the control switch. One of the executioners says to the other, "The contact points must be dirty . . . just click it up and down a few times." Another cartoon depicts a botched-up western-style lynching. Instead of the man hanging by a noose from a tree, we see the horse, the man, and one of the helpers all entangled in the rope and all suspended in midair. The caption reads, "Okay, okay, okay. . . . Everyone just calm down and we'll try this thing one more time."

Perhaps the most prolific laugh-maker to show us that we can laugh at death is Woody Allen. "Birth is a fatal disease," he says. Allen knows, as we all do, that some day we will die. Most of us, however, choose not to discuss it until it confronts us. But Allen bombards us with funny lines while he is questioning his own fear of death—and thereby gets us to look at our own. "It's not that I'm afraid to die," he states, "I just don't want to be there when it happens."

Allen opens the door to a taboo subject and gets us to laugh at our own death by juxtaposing life's unanswerable questions with the nitty-gritty of daily living. Seriousness suddenly becomes ridiculously unserious. "I don't know if I believe in an afterlife, but I am taking a change of underwear just in case." By combining the known with the unknown, Allen puts us on familiar terms with our enemy.

In Allen's short play *Death Knocks*, Death enters the bedroom of Nat Ackerman by climbing in the window and tripping on the windowsill. Death's opening line is, "Jesus Christ, I nearly broke my neck."

Death is no longer a grim reaper but instead a clumsy, out-of-breath entity not unlike the main character. Death has come to take Nat away, but Nat protests, "How can it be the moment? I just merged with Modiste Originals!"

So Nat and Death make a deal. They will play one game of gin. If Nat wins, Death will come back tomorrow; if Death wins, Nat has to go with him. Naturally, Nat wins and Death hastily exists, tripping down the stairs. Death, Nat proclaims, is "such a schlep."

Because Ackerman does not recognize the power of Death, it has no power over him. Similarly, by joking about our own demise, we too can make it—or any of our losses, for that matter—less oppressive.

Through humor, Allen shows us how absurd our here-one-minute, gone-the-next existence is. He even gets us to laugh at our ridiculousness in trying to avoid death. In his film

Sleeper, he pokes fun at both cryogenics, the freezing of the body to preserve life, and cloning, the duplication of body cells. After being awakened from an almost 200-year deep freeze, Allen blurts out, "My doctor said I'd be in the hospital five days. My doctor was 195 years off." Later in the film, Allen mocks an attempt to duplicate the dead commander of the country by cloning him from the only part of the leader that still exists, his nose.

In all of his writing, Allen repeatedly asks, "What is the meaning of life and why are we here?" Although he answers that "life is divided into the horrible and the miserable," underneath his gloom he knows that the only way out of our suffering is with humor.

In *Hannah and Her Sisters*, Allen plays a character who hits bottom and does not want to go on living. Hopelessly depressed, he roams aimlessly around the streets of New York. In a need to sit down, he wanders into a movie theater. There, the images on the screen give him renewed hope and the strength to continue. While viewing the antics of a Marx Brothers film, he realizes that he must stop searching for answers to life's unanswerable questions and start to enjoy himself.

This same message is given to us in another of his films, *Love and Death*. Although it reveals more of Allen's death fears than any of his other works, its main theme is about the need to live fully in spite of our ultimate loss. "You must not allow yourself to be consumed with grief," advises one of the characters. "The dead are dead; life is for the living."

In the last image of this movie, Allen shows us how to live and how to face the end of life. Here we see the main character, Boris, dancing side by side with Death. This image, says Allen's biographer, Maurice Yacowar, "is telling us that in the face of our mortality, we can do nothing better than snap our fingers, dance, laugh, and be hearty. . . ."

LESSONS FROM THOSE WHO KNOW

In this sad world of ours, sorrow comes to all. . . .
It comes with bitterest agony. . . .
Perfect relief is not possible, except with time.
And yet this is a mistake.
You are sure to be happy again,
To know this, which is certainly true,
Will make you [be]come less miserable now.
I have experienced enough to know what I say.

Abraham Lincoln

In his book *Grist for the Mill*, Ram Dass writes about a young woman with four children who was dying of cancer. She asked the participants at a workshop she was attending, "How would you feel if you came into a hospital room to visit a twenty-eight-year-old mother dying of cancer?" The audience called out a host of answers: angry, sad, frustrated, full of pity, confused, horrified. Then she asked, "How would you feel if you were that twenty-eight-year-old mother and everyone who came to visit felt that way?"

Experiencing a serious illness is bad enough. Continually focusing on it makes matters worse. It is of vital importance that as a patient, as a care-giver, or as someone who is concerned about the welfare of the patient, we remain uplifted and keep a positive attitude that includes hope, joy, and laughter even during the most trying of times. Without it, we not only bring ourselves farther down than we already are, but we also drag others down with us.

Mark Feldman, one of the first AIDS patients in this country, showed others with life-threatening illnesses how to remain positive in negative times. On the day he received his diagnosis, he left his doctor's office and realized that he could either handle his illness with love, dignity, and humor or go and hide under a rock. He chose love, dignity, and humor.

Mark went out and got himself a gold spray-painted king's crown to remind him that he was still in charge of his life, that all his power had not been taken away. He knew that he had little control over the course of his disease, but he could control his feelings. "I've decided to put on a happy face," Mark said, "to adopt a cheerful attitude." He began to see all of his tedious medical procedures as games. Whenever he had to climb onto the hospital examination table, for example, he would pretend that he was on the ceiling looking down at what was happening. When I asked why, he said, "It's more fun that way."

Mark is no longer living, but his playful attitude has been an inspiration for many. When asked how people were treating him, after he became ill, he noted, "All of my friends have been just great. They do anything I ask—but I don't understand, nobody wants to do floors or windows."

One woman who has had cancer for seven years called me after her doctor reprimanded her because she did not follow his instructions. She felt let down and contemplated suicide. If her doctor did not care about her, why should she bother to live? The hopelessness was clear in her voice; she felt abandoned.

What turned our conversation around was her discovery that, if nothing else, she had a choice. Perhaps she could not stop her cancer or control her relationship with her doctor. She did, however, have the power to view these situations as she chose. She could see her doctor as being uncaring and her struggle with cancer as an endless, fruitless battle. On the other hand, she could also take a different viewpoint. She could see life through the eyes of a child. See beauty in the smallest detail. Find amazement in the most mundane occurrence. She could smile at a passing butterfly. Only she had the power to discover the wonder in a seemingly wonderless world. Only she had the power to choose each moment anew.

As we spoke, she began to feel stronger. She realized that all was not hopeless. In regaining her power to choose, she was regaining life. And although she was not quite ready to laugh, she now saw the world differently.

Adults can learn a lot from other adults who handle their pain with less suffering, but the best source for this is children. They seem to have an incredible knack for overcoming suffering. Adults could learn a lot about lightening up the dying process from them.

One man I interviewed, Forrest, spoke of the time, just before his daughter was to be examined, that she blew up a surgical glove and put it under her hospital gown with a note that read "Hi, doctor!" He recalls, "I came into the room an hour or so after the incident and the room was so clear. There was no pathos; there was no gloom. It was difficult to describe, other than it was *alive.*"

In a letter Forrest wrote to a friend, he says,

> One would think that it would be a *sad* experience—life on a pediatric ward—but it was *not.* In fact, it is the cheeriest place in the world, because as children always do, they create *fun* for themselves; their business is to deal with their pain first, and then to get on with their *real* business, which is to find joy.

Forrest concluded, "They weren't cancer patients or dying children; they were just children who had cancer."

One of the most inspiring sources on how not to become the victim of our situations comes from the Center for Attitudinal Healing in Tiburon, California. Here Dr. Gerald Jampolsky works mostly with children who have life-threatening illnesses. Rather than bemoan this fact, the children have chosen to make light of it. For example, they respond to questions about the baldness caused by chemotherapy treatments by saying, "God gave some people perfectly shaped heads; the rest he gave hair."

In a book written and illustrated by the children of the center, entitled *There Is a Rainbow Behind Every Dark Cloud*, they declare, "You can learn to control your mind and decide to be happy 'inside' with a smiling heart, in spite of what happens to you on the 'outside.'"

CHAPTER 5

A Happy Ending

To weep too much for the dead is to affront the living.
Proverb

THE CELEBRATION OF LOSS

Funerals are generally grim and solemn affairs. I believe that they can be more than that. If we can allow, and perhaps even plan for, some lighter moments in these ceremonies, they can begin to be more of a celebration for a life lived rather than just the mourning of a life lost. If we can find some celebration in funerals, then, as in life itself, they might include both laughter and tears, not just the latter.

Author Stanley Keleman points out that "at each turning point we have a chance to either make a new myth for ourselves or follow an old one." If we believe that death must be solemn, then that is the way we treat it. If we believe that humor has no place in our suffering or losses, then that is the way we react. But, on the other hand, if we believe that it is possible to maintain an attitude of lightness toward everything in life, including the more difficult segments like death and dying, then that is what we can begin to create for ourselves.

At the end of Dostoevsky's *The Brothers Karamazov*, a young man dies. One of his friends, Alyosha, reminds the rest that after a funeral, the custom is to eat pancakes. The purpose of this is to mix a little sweetness with the bitterness of death.

Perhaps we not only need to add the sweetness of laughter

195

to our memorial ceremonies to help ease the bitter taste of death but also add some humor to them so they become a celebration of life.

The Talmud, an ancient collection of writings that make up Jewish law, teaches this unique lesson:

> Two ships sailed in a harbor: one going out on a voyage, the other coming into port. People cheered the ship going out, but the ship sailing in was hardly noticed. Seeing this, a wise man remarked: "Do not rejoice for a ship sailing out to sea, for you do not know what terrible dangers it may encounter. Rejoice rather for the ship that has reached shore, bringing its passengers safely home."
>
> And so it is in the world. When a child is born, all rejoice; when someone dies, all weep. But it makes just as much sense, if not more, to rejoice at the end of a life as at the beginning. For no one can tell what events await a newborn child, but when a mortal dies he has successfully completed a journey.

We can rejoice when life's journey is over by lightening up our overserious funeral services. First, we can learn how to do this from others who add a little bit of sweetness to their memorials. Second, we can keep an ear open for the spontaneous laughter that often erupts during such high-stress times. And third, we can set the stage for laughter by incorporating some of the humorous characteristics of the deceased in our tributes to them.

MIX SOME SWEET WITH THE BITTER

While walking around the streets of San Francisco one day, I noticed two signs in someone's window that had been taken from a funeral procession. One simply read FUNERAL. The other had originally said the same thing, but someone had cut it apart and rearranged the letters. It read REAL FUN.

In no way am I saying that funerals need be "real fun"; replacing genuine sorrow with false laughter is indeed foolish. Allowing for some humor in a somber occasion, however, helps connect people and provide a balance in time of sorrow. "I think it's true," says cartoonist Bil Keane, "that in any time where you have tragedy, you can get closer together and feel a lot better about the situation if you can laugh at it."

In ancient Rome, the court jester followed the funeral procession of his dead emperor in an effort to lighten up the public ceremony. In present times, a number of cultures around the world incorporate laughter and joy as an intricate part of their death and grieving ceremonies.

The Balinese, for example, believe that the body is just a housing for the spirit. Therefore, when someone dies, it is time of great celebration, because the spirit is finally set free. Their cremation ceremonies are among their most joyous events. Anthropologist Miguel Covarrubias gives us a taste of the elaborateness of this ritual:

> Hundreds of people in a wild stampede carry the beautiful towers, sixty feet high, solidly built of wood and bamboo and decorated with tinsel and expensive silk, in which the bodies are transported to the cremation grounds. There the corpses are placed in great cows (hewn out of tree trunks to serve as coffins and covered with precious materials), and cows, towers, offerings, and ornaments are set on fire, hundreds and even thousands of dollars burned in one afternoon in a mad splurge of extravagance by a people who value the necessities of life in fractions of pennies.

One reporter described a Balinese cremation ceremony as a small Rose Bowl Parade with an Irish wake thrown in for spice.

In Mexico, a Day of the Dead is set aside each year to poke fun at death. Grinning skull cakes, dancing skeletons, and sugar-coated coffin replicas all become part of a ritual to not only remind the living of their mortality but also give them a chance to mock, scorn, and laugh at death.

Laughter takes our minds off our troubles. It diverts our attention and gives us a breather when things are getting too difficult to handle. It distracts us and keeps us occupied so that time, if nothing else, can heal our wounds.

Perhaps no culture has a more raucous way of taking their minds off loss than the Irish. "Let me tell you what Irish wakes are like in my family," said one person. "You cry all the way to the funeral and you laugh all the way back."

In *Trinity*, Leon Uris gives us a glimpse of what goings-on might take place in and around an Irish household where a body has been laid out.

With the heavy lamenting over for a time, the older folks tucked in their niches, smoking away on clay pipes, playing cards and telling stories. Some of the young wanes capered about stuffing pepper into the teapots and tobacco jars, setting off sneezing seizures, while outside the bachelor boys and spinster girls snuck into the shadows to play kissing games and perform mock marriages. There was a group of troublemakers too gawky to mix with girls who amused themselves by a water fight right in the best room, and just near the corpse a group of older men engaged in a dexterity contest, holding a broom handle in both hands and leaping back and forth through it. Directly opposite them, on the far side of the corpse, a dozen women knelt in prayer and keening. The water fight took on a heightened dimension with the addition of potatoes as missiles which buzzed alarmingly close to the worshipers. Just outside, Donall MacDervitt, Finola's cousin from the next village, passed around a bottle of ether to a group lifting weights and leaping a stone wall. In a matter of minutes they were tore out of their minds, staggering crazy and doubled up laugh-

ing like maniacs and thinking they was birds trying to fly off
the roof or over the wall, bashing themselves fearfully but
feeling nary a thing. Someone broke out a fiddle and bag-
pipe and them that wasn't singing revolutionary songs
kicked up their heels in a jig, and the widow women were
getting their juices stirred looking over the eligibles in a
way that spelled no good at all. Arguing broke out over
arguable subjects, which covered just about anything. . . .
Ah, it was a grand wake, a grand wake indeed. Had he not
been dead, Kilty would have been the proudest man alive,
surely he was making an impression on St. Peter and all the
angels for having so many darling friends.

LISTEN FOR SPONTANEOUS LAUGHTER

Laughter has a definite place in times of grief. Like tears, it can
relieve an accumulation of pent-up emotions. During funerals,
however, people often repress laughter because they feel it is
inappropriate, or they feel guilty for disrupting such a solemn
occasion.

Indeed, laughter may not be appropriate if it does not take
the bereaved into consideration. As with other times, we need
to remember to include people in our laughter, not exclude
them.

The very fact that laughter is repressed, however, often
leads to spontaneous hilarity during funerals. Spontaneous laughter, of course, cannot be planned. But, because of
laughter's ability to release tension, it also should not be
shunned.

Nationally syndicated columnist Ann Landers once wrote
about trying to hide spontaneous laughter at her mother's
funeral:

Clergymen who deliver eulogies sometimes become carried
away in a tidal wave of extravagant metaphors. In his at-

tempt to dramatize our mother's indomitable spirit and majestic qualities, the rabbi referred to her as "Rebecca the battleship." My twin sister Popo ["Dear Abby"] looked at me in astonishment and we both began to laugh. We reached for our handkerchiefs to cover our faces. After all, to be seen laughing at one's mother's funeral is not considered acceptable behavior.

Our two older sisters, Dorothy and Helen, also were stunned by the battleship reference. When they saw us, our faces buried in our handkerchiefs, they, too, began to laugh. Meanwhile, observers could not figure out why the four Friedman girls were simultaneously overcome with grief. . . .

Philosophers have told us through the ages that comedy and tragedy are separated by a very thin line. The same is true of laughter and tears. On that hot day in Sioux City, it all became perfectly clear.

It has been said that man is often the funniest when he least means to be. As exemplified in the story above, laughter frequently arises from incongruous statements made at the most solemn of times. What we need to learn is not to suppress our laughter when these incongruities occur. We need to acknowledge that something funny has been said and not feel guilty because we are laughing.

J. Terryl Bechtol, owner of a funeral home near Pensacola, Florida, tells another humorous story involving incongruities. It took place at his establishment and is one that he says he will never forget.

We had a funeral of an elderly man who had many grandchildren. The room was full and the widow was not handling things too well. She kept saying, "He just doesn't look right, he just doesn't look natural." Everyone in the room was quite uneasy, and the funeral director was trying to tell her that this was the best that could be done, and he looked quite well, but she said once again, in a rather loud voice, "He just doesn't look right." The room became silent! At that moment, her six-year-old grandson looked up at her and said, "Of course, he don't look natural, Grandma, you ain't never seen him dead before!"

After the initial gasp from everyone in the room, Grandma burst out laughing and everyone else in the room did too.

An inadvertently said word or two is sometimes all it takes to turn tears to laughter. We cannot plan for these, but we can keep our ears open for them and thereby help relieve some of the tension found at funerals.

Cliff Thomas, "the Philosophical Pharmacist" from South Dakota, shares one such story about some inadvertent words that were spoken at his uncle's funeral.

Uncle Tom was laid out in his best suit and, as was the custom, he had the large blue ribbon with the gold braid and name tag pinned on that read "St. Patrick's Parish Holy Name Society." At Catholic funerals the deceased usually have one of these pinned to them—it was blue with gold frills, about two inches wide and five inches long.

Slightly flustered, Aunt Mary reached into the casket and began adjusting Uncle Tom's coat, which really needed no adjustment.

I said, "Why are you doing that, Aunt Mary?"

She replied, "He doesn't look good. His coat is wrinkled."

I said, "What do you mean, he doesn't look good—he looks great. In fact, it looks to me like he won first prize!"

My comment immediately broke the tension in the room. I even saw Uncle Tom smile.

Another story, this told by Robert Henry, a professional humorist from Alabama, illustrates again how a couple of humorous words can bring someone out of deepest sorrow.

Mother and I had a very unusual relationship. She was my best friend, my biggest fan, and my greatest encouragement. In 1976 she died.

With me at the time was mother's best friend, Nell. Mother had told Nell that I would probably throw a fit when it came time for her to go to the Lord, so Nell had better stay close by me.

I have never felt such an overwhelming burden when mother died. It was as if the world had suddenly crashed on my shoulders. I did not think I could stand it; I felt like I was going to die too. As I stood to move away from her bedside, suddenly my knees began to get away from me. I felt like I had been hit. Like a boxer might be hit. I didn't think I could stand. In an effort to get up, I managed to put my arm around Nell, who was about 5' 6" and weighed maybe 120 pounds, while I was 6' 2" and weighed 285 pounds. I looked down at her and said, "Nell, I think I'm going to faint." She looked up at me and said, "What do you do when you faint?"

What Nell meant was, Do I put cold compresses on your head? Do I pat your cheek? Do I elevate your feet? But here is the way the exchange went:

I said, "Nell, I think I am going to faint." She said, "What do you do when you faint?" And I answered, "I fall on my butt."

Now, at a time in my life when I have never known such a burden, such oppression, such grief, the humorist in me came to the fore. At this time, at the most horrible moment in my life, it was humor that gave me the strength to get over that terrible moment I was experiencing.

SET THE STAGE FOR HUMOR

If introduced in the right way, the stage can be deliberately set for some cathartic laughter during a funeral ceremony. Robert Orben, for example, says he knows of a minister who always tries to include the favorite joke of the deceased in the eulogy. It serves as a temporary respite from grief and also beings back warm memories of happier times with the loved one.

Jokes are only one way to add humor to a funeral and not one that I would readily recommend. (Although one study did show that the audience was *not* upset with the eulogist even when inappropriate jokes were told.) Without running the risk of possibly offending with a joke, ceremonies for the deceased can be designed to allow humor to emerge naturally.

What I am suggesting is that in planning a funeral, look for and incorporate humor that best expresses the characteristics of the deceased. Laura said that at her mother's funeral, for example, rather than have formal speeches, a friend invited people to talk about some of the fond times they had shared with the deceased. An atmosphere was created that allowed people to say things that were not so solemn. One person got up and told of the time her mother jokingly brought some bread to a baby shower that was formed in the shape of male and female genitals. Another person went up to the coffin and told the corpse an off-color story. "Your mother would have really liked that one," he said.

In his biography of Harvey Milk, the San Francisco supervisor who was murdered, author Randy Shilts describes another unusual funeral service. Milk's box of ashes was wrapped in "Doonesbury" comics, one of his favorites, and the initials R.I.P. were spelled out in rhinestones across the box. His ashes were scattered into the ocean along with purple Kool-Aid and bubble bath. The lavender cascade of bubbles was a fitting end for a homosexual public official who often equated politics with theater and who had a flair for the dramatic.

In *The American Way of Death*, writer Jessica Mitford questions the appropriateness of ceremonies that go to great lengths to display a lifeless corpse. I believe that it would be more fitting, and perhaps less somber, if memorial ceremonies not only incorporated some of the humorous qualities of the deceased but also took place in surroundings that had closer connections to them.

In this final suggestion of how to set the stage for humor at a funeral, the Reverend Robert Cromey from San Francisco speaks of a service at which he officiated:

> I'd like to tell you about a funeral/memorial I conducted not long ago in the Boarding House, a San Francisco nightclub. It was for Rollin Newton.
>
> Seventy-five friends and relatives gathered. I sat on a bar stool in front of the gathering of a mixed group of grievers. The ancient psalms pleaded where comics give their pitch. The stately Anglican prayer pushed into the space where the crash of rock and roll music hovered. The fears and choked voices of the mourners blended into the air where wild laughter soon would pervade.
>
> People talked of Rollin's humor, technical ability as a sound man, his singing and guitar playing, his neighborliness and kindness in helping people into business.
>
> I told the people that a memorial service in a workplace was incredibly appropriate. In that club Rollin Newton worked. His skill and energy were expended in that place. The gospel of resurrection and new life is real in this place where people laugh, relax, eat, drink, and make merry. It is apparent in this man's work, life, and friends. . . .
>
> The work of a priest is wonderful—full of wonder. My first nightclub performance was a memorial service. It was beautiful, wondrous, and a privilege.

When I die, I want all my friends and family to celebrate. I want each to have a jar of bubbles and blow them in the air as a symbol of the beauty and the fleeting aspect of life. And I want them to remember, and be comforted by, the Talmudic line quoted earlier: "It makes just as much sense, if not more, to rejoice at the end of life as at the beginning."

A Feather for Your Thoughts

Life is risky; we are all acrobats
Tiptoeing over one bridge or another.
To a tightrope walker
The rope is just like home.
Those who hold their bodies lightly
And their minds simply
May seem in danger
But they are safe.

Chinese scrolls

One of the most important teachers in my life has been a man named Stephen Levine. He conducts death-and-dying workshops and has written a number of books, including *Who Dies?* and *Healing into Life and Death.* Although Levine works in the field of death and dying, he is not only addressing our ultimate loss but all loss, and not only loss, but living.

When Levine said, "As long as death is the enemy, life is a struggle," I realized that as long as any of my losses and upsets are my enemy, then they continually cause me pain. I cannot allow my losses to be any more special than they are. When I get caught up in my sorrow, I am taking a tragic stance. When I can "keep my heart open in hell," to use one of Stephen's quotes, then I am ready for anything, even laughter.

From time to time, I have mentioned "using humor." We

do not really "use" humor, but we can allow it to happen—to be open to it, to see it and not push it away or try and force it. It is what Levine calls "allowing an openness to the absurdity of the moment."

With this openness, you can learn to laugh again even after the most painful experience, but it takes time. Mark Twain said that relatives who overstay their welcome cannot just be thrown out the window, but must be coaxed a step at a time toward the door.

Be gentle with yourself and your loss. Move your pain slowly out the door with the perspective of humor.

In closing, I would like to share part of an article by Barbara Stacy from *East West* journal about a child whom Dr. Gerald Jampolsky met at Baptist Hospital in Jacksonville, Florida:

> She was only six, and she had had liver biopsies, bone biopsies—you name it. But it was as if none of that stuff had ever happened. She was one of the happiest kids in the world, giving her love and light away. I had just met with the hospital administrator, who was dealing with a major conflict between the medical and surgical departments. I said to Angela, "See that guy? He's sad right now because some people are upset with him. . . . Can you say something that might help him?" . . . She put her hand to her face. "Oh, mister, I know what you could do. Go out and buy a feather and tickle him three times a day." I sent this administrator a feather and told him the story. And on days when I'm overly serious, I use my imagination and tickle myself with a feather and think of Angela.

If I had my way, there would be a feather on the last page of this book, as a reminder to you to keep things light.

BIBLIOGRAPHY

In addition to the books listed below, there are hundreds of others filled with jokes, anecdotes, and cartoons. If you are interested in these, go to either a bookstore or a library and begin looking up such people as Steve Allen, Woody Allen, Teresa Bloomingdale, Erma Bombeck, Ashleigh Brilliant, Art Buchwald, Bennett Cerf, Gary Larson, Robert Orben, and Larry Wilde.

Bach, Richard. *Illusions.* New York: Dell Publishing, 1979.

Basso, Bob, with Judi Klosek. *Lighten Up, Corporate America!* Los Angeles: New Breed Publications, 1986.

Blumenfeld, Esther, and Lynne Alpern. *The Smile Connection.* Englewood Cliffs, NJ: Prentice-Hall, 1986.

Bonham, Tal D. *Humor: God's Gift.* Nashville: Broadman Press, 1988.

Bresler, David E., and Richard Turbo. *Free Yourself from Pain.* New York: Simon & Schuster, 1979.

Center for Attitudinal Healing. *There Is a Rainbow Behind Every Dark Cloud.* Millbrae, CA: Celestial Arts, 1978.

Chapman, Antony, and Hugh Foot, eds. *Humour and Laughter: Theory, Research and Applications.* London: Wiley & Sons, 1976.

Cousins, Norman. *Anatomy of an Illness.* New York: W. W. Norton & Co., 1979.

Diamond, John. *Your Body Doesn't Lie.* New York: Warner, 1979.

Dyer, Wayne. *The Sky's the Limit.* New York: Pocket Books, 1980.

Eberhart, E. T. *In the Presence of Humor: A Guide to the Humorous Life.* Salem, OR: Pilgrim House, 1983.

Farrelly, Frank, and Jeff Brandsma. *Provocative Therapy.* Cupertino, CA: META Publications, 1974.

Fay, Allen. *Making Things Better by Making Them Worse.* New York: Hawthorn Books, 1978.

Fisher, Seymour and Rhoda Fisher. *Pretend the World Is Funny and Forever.* Hillsdale, NJ: L. Eribaum, 1981.

Frankl, Victor E. *Man's Search for Meaning.* New York: Simon & Schuster, 1963.

Frey, William, and Muriel Langsath. *Crying: The Mystery of Tears.* New York: Harper & Row, 1985.

Fry, William F., Jr., and Melanie Allen. *Make 'em Laugh: Life Studies of Comedy Writers.* Palo Alto, CA: Science and Behavior Books, 1975.

Fry, William F., Jr., and Waleed A. Salameh, eds. *Handbook of Humor and Psychotherapy.* Sarasota, FL: Professional Resource Exchange, 1986.

Goodman, Joel, ed. *Laughing Matters* magazine. Saratoga Springs, NY: The HUMOR Project, 1983 to present.

Grotjahn, Martin. *Beyond Laughter: Humor and the Subconscious.* New York: McGraw-Hill, 1957.

Gruner, Charles. *Understanding Laughter: The Workings of Wit and Humor.* Chicago: Nelson-Hall, 1978.

Hyers, Conrad. *Zen and the Comic Spirit.* Philadelphia: Westminster, 1974.

Keller, Dan. *Humor as Therapy.* Wauwatosa, WI: Pine Mountain Press, 1984.

Kuhlman, Thomas. *Humor and Psychotherapy.* Homewood, IL: Dow Jones–Irwin, 1984.

Kushner, Harold. *When Bad Things Happen to Good People.* New York: Shocken Books, 1981.

Lerner, Helene, with Roberta Elins. *Stress Breakers.* Minneapolis: CompCare Publishers, 1985.

McCormack, Mark H. *What They Don't Teach You at Harvard Business School.* New York: Bantam Books, 1984.

McGhee, Paul E. *Humor: Origins and Development.* San Francisco: W. H. Freeman and Co., 1979.

McGhee, Paul E., and Jeffrey H. Goldstein. *The Handbook of Humor Research.* 2 vols. New York: Springer-Verlig, 1983.

Mendel, Werner, ed. *A Celebration of Laughter.* Los Angeles: Mara Books, 1970.

Mikes, George. *Laughing Matter: Towards a Personal Philosophy of Wit and Humor.* New York: Library Press, 1971.

Mindess, Harvey. *Laughter and Liberation.* Los Angeles: Nash Publishing Co., 1971.

Moody, Raymond, Jr. *Laugh after Laugh.* Jacksonville, FL: Headwaters Press, 1978.

Nahemow, Lucille, et al., eds. *Humor and Aging.* Orlando, FL: Academic Press, Inc., 1982.

Novak, William, and Moshe Waldoks, eds. *The Big Book of Jewish Humor.* New York: Harper & Row, 1981.

Peter, Laurence J., and Bill Dana. *The Laughter Prescription.* New York: Ballantine Books, 1982.

Plessner, Helmuth. *Laughing and Crying.* Evanston, IL: Northwestern University Press, 1970.

Prather, Hugh. *Notes to Myself.* Moab, Utah: Real People Press, 1970.

Reps, Paul, ed. *Zen Flesh, Zen Bones.* Rutland, VT: Charles E. Tuttle Company, 1957.

Robinson, Vera M. *Humor and the Health Professions.* Thorofare, NJ: Charles B. Slack Company, 1977.

Sheehy, Gail. *Pathfinders.* New York: Bantam Books, 1981.

Siegel, Bernie. *Love, Medicine and Miracles.* New York: Harper & Row, 1986.

Simonton, O. Carl, Stephanie Matthews-Simonton, and James Creighton. *Getting Well Again.* Los Angeles: J. P. Tarcher, 1978.

True, Herb, and Anna Mang. *Humor Power: How to Get It, Give It, and Gain.* Garden City, NY: Doubleday, 1980.

Vaillant, George. *Adaption to Life.* Boston: Little, Brown, and Co., 1977.

Viorst, Judith. *Necessary Losses.* New York: Ballantine Books, 1986.

Von Oech, Roger. *A Kick in the Seat of the Pants,* New York: Perennial Press, 1986.

Waitley, Denis, and Reni L. Witt. *The Joy of Working.* New York: Ballantine Books, 1986.

Weinstein, Matt, and Joel Goodman. *Playfair: Everybody's Guide to Non-Competitive Play.* San Luis Obispo, CA: Impact Publishers, 1980.

Yacowar, Maurice. *Loser Take All: The Comic Art of Woody Allen.* New York: Frederick Unger Publishing, 1979.

Ziv, Avner. *Personality and Sense of Humor.* New York: Springer, 1984.